ADVAITIC SĀDHANĀ

OR

THE YOGA OF DIRECT LIBERATION

ADVAITIC SĀDHANĀ

or

The Yoga of Direct Liberation

Containing English Translations of
Māṇḍūkyopaniṣad and Ātma Bodha

S. S. COHEN

MOTILAL BANARSIDASS PUBLISHERS
PRIVATE LIMITED • DELHI

Reprint: Delhi, 2011
First Edition: Delhi, 1975

ISBN: 978-81-208-3171-1

MOTILAL BANARSIDASS
41 U.A. Bungalow Road, Jawahar Nagar, Delhi 110 007
8 Mahalaxmi Chamber, 22 Bhulabhai Desai Road, Mumbai 400 026
236, 9th Main III Block, Jayanagar, Bangalore 560 011
203 Royapettah High Road, Mylapore, Chennai 600 004
Sanas Plaza, 1302 Baji Rao Road, Pune 411 002
8 Camac Street, Kolkata 700 017
Ashok Rajpath, Patna 800 004
Chowk, Varanasi 221 001

By arrangement with
Sri Ramanasramam
Tiruvannamalai 606 603,
Tamil Nadu INDIA

Typset at
Sri Ramanasramam

Printed in India
at SRI VENKATESA PRINTING HOUSE, CHENNAI 600 026
AND PUBLISHED BY NARENDRA PRAKASH JAIN FOR
MOTILAL BANARSIDASS PUBLISHERS PRIVATE LIMITED,
BUNGALOW ROAD, DELHI 110 007

PUBLISHER'S NOTE

We are delighted to make available to seekers this succinct trilogy on *Advaitic Sādhanā*, which in itself constitutes a thorough, practical guide on the path to Self-realisation. The author, S. S. Cohen, spent many years at the feet of his Master, Sri Ramana Maharshi, and devoted his entire life to the fulfilment of the teachings he had absorbed.

BOOK I of this work has particular relevance to spiritual aspirants visiting Sri Ramanasramam, as it was written for them in the 1940s with the sole aim of making their visit to Sri Ramana Maharshi fruitful. These same guidelines and insights presented by the author are as relevant now as they were then.

S. S. Cohen was absorbed in his Master on May 27, 1980. His *samādhi* tomb lies within the Ashram premises and annually his life is ceremoniously remembered on this date.

14 May 2007
57th Aradhana Day

PUBLISHER
SRI RAMANASRAMAM

To

SRI RAMANA OF ARUNACHALA

The Supreme Lord of Advaita

PREFACE

This book is a small trilogy on the science of Self-knowledge, a science which has been from time immemorial inculcated in this country by the great Vedantic Masters to those who sat at their feet, seeking release from the misery of birth and death and succeeded. Its greatest exponent in our own age, who lived more then half a century in our midst, was the celebrated sage Ramana of Arunachala, who left behind him a compendious literature which benefited thousands of truth seekers all the world over and led a number of them to final and complete Emancipation.

The trilogy consists of (1) *Advaitic Sādhanā* or the Yoga of Direct Liberation,which throws much light on the practice of *sādhanā*, especially meditation, (2) The well known *Māṇḍūkya Upaniṣad* with brief notes and (3) *Ātma Bodha* of Śaṅkara, the greatest expounder of the Upaniṣads, with simple comments bringing out the meaning of the stanzas, in simple language, comprehensible even to foreign beginners.

Vellore, 1975 S. S. C.

CONTENTS

Preface ix

BOOK I — Advaitic Sādhanā xiii
Introductory xv
Chapters
1 The Qualified Disciple 1
2 Necessity of Sādhanā 5
3 Dhyāna (Meditation) 9
4 Pitfalls 20
5 Samādhi 22
6 The Sāttvic Food 24
7 Sādhakās 27
8 Conclusion 31

BOOK II — Māṇḍūkyopaniṣad 33
Introductory 35
Śruti I to XII 37-52

BOOK III — Ātma Bodha 53
Introductory 55
Stanza 1 to 68 57-92

INDEX 93

INTRODUCTORY

This essay was drafted many years ago, when the author was residing in Sri Ramanasramam at Tiruvannamalai in the gracious presence of his Master, Sri Ramana Maharshi, where many foreigners used to flock on short visits. He used to watch their comings and goings and the haste with which most of them expected to pluck the plum of Self-realisation, immediate apprehension of the Reality, before even grasping the elementary principles of the Master's teaching or the Vedantic truth. It is especially for their benefit that this treatise has been written.

The term "Direct Liberation" used in the subtitle seeks, as in the *Bhāgavata Purāṇa*, to distinguish the "direct" path of the *Jñāna Mārga* (the path of immediate knowledge), whereby Liberation is gained and the essence of bliss tasted by the *Paramahaṁsas* in this very life, from the "indirect" path, which is said to take several million years spent in a disembodied state by the *Haṁsas* in a number of subtle spheres and results from the practice of *prāṇāyāma* (breathing exercises), ritualistic and devotional worship (*upāsana*), etc.

CHAPTER 1

THE QUALIFIED DISCIPLE

THIS is the age of shortcuts. Time has shrunk and space more so, and the dual inconvenience has affected men's moods and temper. Even the supreme Knowledge has nowadays to be given in massive doses and has to produce quick results too, or they will have none of it.

In olden days *Brahmajñāna* (the knowledge of the Absolute) used to be imparted by the *Ṛṣis* (Self-realised sages) to their *sannyāsi* (world renouncer) disciples *only* over a number of years. Staying with the Guru in seclusion, often in the forest, for the whole of the period was a prerequisite for many good reasons, which the disciples could not question. Now we cannot do that: time presses and our patience has, likewise, suffered contraction, so has our appreciation of the quest and the prize at issue.

Besides, the culture which most of us have inherited is too extroverted and too aggressively intellectual to permit us to understand within a short time what it all means to be a *sādhakā*, a practical aspirant for a truth of which in our homes and colleges we were not given an inkling. We are apt, moreover, to bring with us scraps of knowledge gleaned from a wide reading of miracle-ridden theology and "occultism", including an endeavour to accommodate the Vedānta inside them. The result is that we return from the Guru (the qualified Teacher) and his Ashram with our doubts still in our heads, uncleared, and our minds, about truth and untruth, still befogged.

It is necessary at the outset to understand that it is not possible to hound out *avidyā* (the primeval ignorance arising out of the sense-perceptions) with a half-hearted approach, with scanty faith, with a mind weighed down by preconceptions, stubborn worldliness, fixed ideas and inordinate haste. These do not qualify for the Supreme Knowledge *(Jñāna),* which exacts a steady, unwavering, whole-hearted discipline.

Authentic seekers are humble and modest in their expectations and do not, as a rule, lay down conditions in advance of their yogic practice, nor fix time as to their possible attainment of the Goal, but surrender themselves unreservedly to their *sādhana* (spiritual discipline) and to the guidance of the Teacher, unmindful of the results.

The seeker of the Absolute must have no object in life but the persistent pursuit of the Absolute, to which he bends all the power of his soul. To approach it in any other attitude, say with motives not strictly spiritual, or with a surfeited, insubordinate intellect, or to expect the Absolute to bend and yield its secrets in the first week or first month for one's own sake, for the sake of one's worldly achievements, illustrious ancestry or community, denotes a lack of the most elementary qualities that make one eligible for it. Eclecticism likewise has no place in this path: its application is poor, its understanding diffused, so are its spiritual yearnings.

It will be observed that this approach attacks the object, that is the world appearance, from two fronts — the one by investigation, which helps distinguish the sentient, changeless seer from the insentient, ever-changing seen, the body; and the other by *dhyāna* (meditation), which suppresses the seen and reveals the seer. With the former we dialectically expose the fallacy and worthlessness of the sense data and, thus, demolish the foundations over which we have been accustomed to raise the false structure of our knowledge, and with the other we dive deep into their substratum to find the subject as he is in himself, the owner of the senses, who is the absolute Reality.

Śaṅkara gives a picturesque description of the aspirant who qualifies for this knowledge and his approach to the Self-realised Teacher in ancient times:

"We shall now explain the method by which Liberation is attained for the benefit of those who aspire for it and who desire to know this method with full faith.

"This means to Liberation, namely, Knowledge, should be explained again and again until it is firmly grasped to a pure *brāhmaṇa* (seeker of Brahman, the absolute) disciple who is indifferent to everything that is transitory; who has given up the desire for a son, for wealth and for this world and the next; who has taken to a life of *sannyāsa* (renunciation and asceticism) and has control over his mind and senses; who possesses compassion and all the qualities of a disciple enjoined by the scriptures, and who has approached the Teacher in the prescribed manner and has been examined in respect of his profession, conduct, learning and parentage."

(*Upadeśasahasrī* – I, 1,1-3)

CHAPTER 2

NECESSITY OF SĀDHANĀ

> The unsteady of mind has no knowledge of the Supreme; nor has he meditation. To the unmeditating there is no peace; and to the unpeaceful how can there be happiness?
>
> (*Bhagavad Gītā, II,* 66)

THESE lines are a philosophy of life in a nutshell: they guide him who desires to live in peace with the world and with himself, as well as him who is bent upon taking the pilgrim's staff in search of the truth absolute and the freedom for which his soul yearns. They tell the former that peace is unattainable without mental steadiness, and the latter that mind control through meditation is absolutely essential to attain that Knowledge which alone can give release.

The mind, which is the only instrument of knowledge man possesses, is usually never at rest and too entangled in the object of desire it perceives and in the duties, responsibilities and attachments which these impose upon it, to know how to release itself from them. The help of the Master becomes necessary to show the way out of the sense mess and into the aloneness of the Being *(kaivalya)*, of the pure mind itself, which is all purity and tranquillity. This is the supreme knowledge to which the following lines refer:

> I know this mighty Being, who shines effulgent like the sun beyond darkness. One triumphs over death only by knowing Him. There is indeed no other way to Liberation. *(Śvetāśvatāra Upaniṣad, III, 8)*

To "triumph over death" discipline of the mind *(sādhanā)* is, therefore, necessary. As in deep sleep the subject enjoys the massive bliss of *kaivalya* when he sees no sights, hears no sounds, and is completely free from thoughts, so must the yogi in the waking state withdraw into the *kaivalya* of himself through meditation to attain the knowledge of the Being or Self, which is the supreme Liberation. This method is called *jñāna mārga* (the path of knowledge) or *jñāna yoga* (the yoga of knowledge). In no system is the practice made so easy and safe as in this yoga, because, first, it is dialectical and, secondly, it is free from the dangers, which often result from misdirected practices which interfere with the natural functions of the body, or with supersensible forces lying beyond the control of the subject himself.

Jñāna yoga, also called *Advaitic Sādhanā* (non-dualistic discipline), is the direct path to Liberation. The process can be summed up in only three words: *Empty your mind.* In dreamless sleep the mind is totally empty of thoughts, plunged as it is in the bliss of its own native state, the pure consciousness *(cit).* But waking is the state of thinking, which projects the worlds of time and space and covers the being, like the dust that covers a clean mirror. In order therefore to perceive this effulgent Being, thoughts have to be arrested; the mirror of the mind has to be cleared of its dust. This is called *Turīya* (the Fourth State, to distinguish it from the other three states of waking, dreaming and deep sleep), which experiences the blissful aloneness of *suṣupti* (deep sleep) in the full view of the waking *(jāgrat),* when the senses and the faculty of cognition are present but rendered inactive by practice. Its other name is *samādhi,* the ecstacy of self-cognition.

It goes without saying that the first attempts to arrest the onrush of thoughts appear frustrating, sometimes even painful, but success is sure to result from persistent efforts. Constant practice releases the mind from its inhibitions, its habits, memories, fear, suppressed longing, anxiety, etc., and establishes a free flow of the *dhyānic* current at the same time every day, if regularity in the practice is scrupulously maintained.

Those who find it difficult to restrain the mind from the very start take to *japa* (repetition of a mantra, or holy name) which is soothing and awe inspiring, preparatory to meditation. The reduction of thoughts to a substantial degree is indispensable for entering the state of *samādhi* and, as this cannot be achieved without mind control, all other methods have eventually to pass into *dhyāna* (meditation), when the mind will be able to stand "like the jet of a lamp that is protected from a breeze" (Patañjali). The *japa* will by then have ceased to be repeated orally, but will have turned into the silent *ajapa,* the serene quietude in the Heart which is the end and aim of *dhyāna*.

Other means of subduing the thinking faculty, such as drugs, breath control to obtain the cataleptic state of *laya,* interference with the uvula and the frenum lingui, etc., do not concern us here. Genuine *sādhakas* (practising yogis) avoid short cuts which may land them in dangerous situations. *Dhyāna* and *vichāra* (meditation and investigation), if done steadily, will not fail to take them safely to the glorious Self. It is not by stupefying or over-exciting the cerebral cells, nor by circumventing the century-old discipline, but by purifying and controlling the mind that the vision of Reality can be ensured.

CHAPTER 3

DHYĀNA (MEDITATION)

WE have seen that *sādhanā* is necessary for those who keenly feel the impermanence and hardships of the world of sense, and seek redemption from them and from the affliction of *avidyā* (ignorance). We have also discussed the nature and results of the *sādhanā* in general. Now we shall examine a few practical methods of *dhyāna* which are known to have helped seekers throughout the centuries to tread the same path and arrive.

I wish first to remark that the failure of many people to lead their *dhyāna* to success is due to two principal causes. First is their inability to concentrate at all, let alone for any appreciable length of time, which induces some of them to resort to makeshifts or follow a Guru who does not recommend *dhyāna*. The second, by far the greater cause, is their starting with inadequate knowledge, with hazy, improperly-formed ideas about the aim and object of their meditation, which naturally results in their remaining in the cloud of uncertainty for a long time. The vast majority of beginners are in too great a haste to take to the road of *dhyāna* before seizing themselves of all its facts and principles. Who is therefore to blame if they feel at a loss to know how to meditate, how to begin meditation, or if the meditation always remains thin and jejune? It is not enough to snatch a few slogans, shut the eyes, and start questioning oneself "Who am I?" or suggesting to oneself "I am not the body nor the senses," etc. A comprehensive grasp of the Master's teaching and profound reflections are absolutely necessary to endow the meditator with a prior knowledge of what he is to expect from the *dhyāna* and the direction it should take, or else who is to answer his questions? For the very mind that asks them is itself the Reality it is seeking, and if it has not been understood with full conviction as such, how can the meditation be clear in its objective to succeed? This is the stage when no one can help the meditator: he has to help himself by assiduous application and deep cogitation on the words of the Master to draw practical conclusions from them, which is itself a sort of meditation and which in course of time matures into the meditation proper, whose aim is to annihilate the *vṛtti* (mind transformation or thoughts) which covers the reality of the Self, as has been explained in the last chapter.

Meditation is a self-contained process, which goes on correcting itself to perfection by trials and errors in him who comes prepared for it. It somehow finds its way by the light of its own torch, catching the smallest hints that rise from within or without and automatically acting on them without even the knowledge of the surface consciousness. The presence of the Guru is then of the greatest help, and must be availed of at any cost, if by then the Guru has revealed himself. If not, dwelling in holy places and clean environments is essential till the Guru is found. In fact, to those who have attained this state of maturity the Guru does not tarry to appear somehow. They are never left in the lurch for long in that respect. He is there waiting, as it were, all the time: the seeking, conscious or unconscious, is definitely mutual.

Residence with the Guru during the whole period of the practice is of inestimable value (occasional absenteeism excepted), for reasons which the *sādhaka* (the practitioner) will not fail to discover by himself after passing the stage of apprenticeship and beginning to know what is what in the true spiritual life. There will be, moreover, no particular inclination on his part to return to the world, if he means business and is truly fervent. The time factor is of the utmost importance to him: he abhors being a minute longer than he can help it in this welter of vanity, superficialities, and wasted efforts. He cannot afford to lead a busy life for pretty nothing, or lead a life of lax indifference. He has by then developed a positive detachment, contemplative habits, love for seclusion and for *sāttvic* (pure) company, particularly that of the Guru. Yet the worldly-mindedness which he brings with him takes a long time to be rubbed off. Its substitution by the *nivṛtti* (return to the being) impressions is made easy by meditative efforts, supplemented by the holiness which ceaselessly emanates from the Guru. Worldly people

ance (*tapas*), of which they are very scared, gining it to call for Herculean efforts and great sacrifices. Nothing is farther from the truth. Apart from the very first steps there exists no suffering worth mentioning for those who are seriously inclined towards it. The suffering seen by others in the *tapasvin* lies only in their own imagination. The *tapasvin* himself enjoys the indescribable bliss of the inner freedom which *tapas* affords — freedom from the terrible load with which the world burdens the ordinary life. The *tapasvin* has thrown down that load and is now free. The strict meaning of *tapas* in this path is adherence to the quest for the Self, and if the Self has already been realised, continued inherence in it, not allowing oneself to slip back again to the world of the senses (*Ramana Gītā,* XI, 19). The true *tapasvin* is he who has, in his heart and mind, turned his back completely to the world. If he has not done that, domestic life is best for him. He will be freer at home than in an Ashram or a temple to pursue his seeking even in the midst of his worldly affairs. It is no use being in an Ashram in seclusion when the instrument through which he expects to attain peace — the mind — is itself disturbed by longings.

It goes without saying that this has nothing whatever in common with the flesh and soul mortifications of the Hindu and Christian extremists, of the cave and desert hermits. The *Bhagavad Gītā* insists on moderation in everything and on the necessity of maintaining good health and mental ease and comfort.

Once the mind is cleared of the dead past it will be amenable to adjust itself to the new conditions. The Guru, let it be at once stated, merely reveals this truth and its import to the *sādhakā* and points the direction to it, but He cannot take the place of the meditation, which is the preparation of the mind for the supreme experience by the yogi himself, no more than the schoolmaster can himself make the study on behalf of his pupils. Nor can the Guru confer the ability to meditate, or, for the matter of that, *mukti* (Liberation) itself by an act of His will. For then there would be no need for any practice whatever, or for even self-purification: who would then take all this trouble when a simple request to the Guru would do the trick? *Sādhanā* would then be a mockery and *mukti* valueless. Moreover, the true Guru is not less than a *jīvanmukta,* one who had divested Himself of all personal volition even prior to His attainment, and, when He had become the one Self, the absolute Brahman, not only the personal will but also the vision of multiplicity, of otherness, had ceased to exist for Him. To ascribe to Him, therefore, partiality and discrimination denotes ignorance, if not also disloyalty to Him. Yet miracles, as acts of His Grace, do sometimes appear, but these are not brought about consciously and deliberately by Him as an individual, but the powers latent in His pure mind mysteriously respond in their own gracious ways, if the *prārabdha* (destiny) of the devotee concerned is favourable.

The impulse and desire for meditation have thus to be born inside the *sādhakā's* own heart, and they are invariably so born when the heart by long-sustained aspirations has sufficiently blossomed and developed an appreciable degree of detachment *(vairāgya)* and the mind has cooperated with it in a rational sensitivity to truth and in a power of discrimination *(viveka)*. The Guru becomes then extremely valuable, not only as a revealer of the Truth and the way to it, but also as an inspiring, purifying and soothing influence which calms the storm which agitates the hearts not yet turned truly ascetic, hastening the maturing of meditation into *samādhi*.

The true seeker goes on plodding with his meditation day in and day out, year in and year out, supplementing it in his free hours with the study of the subject of his meditation, so that his mind may not lie fallow and fall back in its old ruts, or retrospect on incidents the memory of which does decided harm to his *sādhanā*. A careful watch has to be kept on the tricks of the memory which keeps bringing to the present sorrowful and remorseful events and associations, which had better remain buried in the past. Equally distressing is the memory of persons who, in their times, had left profound marks on the heart and mind. All these recollections have to be guarded against and nipped in the bud the moment they make their appearance. The past, in brief, has to be thrown into limbo to preserve the calm which is necessary for the practice.

Once out of the initial darkness the mind becomes eager to receive concrete directions and hints, which throw some light on its journey in this uncharted land of the spirit, which stretches before it to infinity without landmarks or milestones.

We come now to the core of the subject — meditation. What is meditation, and why it is practised? Meditation is simply the repeated attempt to withdraw one's thoughts from the multitudes of objects around and fix them on only one object — the subject chosen for concentration. In chapter two we have dealt with the restlessness and unhappiness of the unrestrained, diffused mind. Although the mind is said to be fleeter than the wind, fleeter than lightning and thus uncontrollable, yet by constant practice it slowly bends and acquires quiescence and depth till it reaches the Heart or Self, which is absolute peace, the mind's own true nature, free from thoughts. This is the true meditation and its aim in this yoga.

To those who are unable to choose their own subjects for concentration the following hints are given.

1. Meditation on the nature of the Being, which is the source and substratum of all thoughts known in the *śrutis* (the revealed scriptures, e.g. Upaniṣads) as the *ākāśa* (ether) of consciousness, or Heart, develops an intuition of it, wearing away all the images from the meditating mind, polishing it and, finally, revealing it to be the shining sun of knowledge, free from the dark cloud of the phenomena (or thoughts) that have hitherto been covering it. Its other names are: *Cit, Caitanya, Ātman, Paramātman* (Pure Mind, Pure Consciousness, Self, Supreme Self), etc. *Śāṇḍilya Upaniṣad* describes this practice graphically thus:

> O Śāṇḍilya, be happy. Place the Self in the midst of the *ākāśa,* and the *ākāśa* in the midst of the Self and, having reduced everything to *ākāśa,* do not think. You will not entertain then either internal or external thoughts. Abandoning all thoughts, become abstract thought itself. As camphor dissolves in fire and salt in water, so does *manas* (the thinking faculty) dissolve in *Tattva* (the Reality). What is termed *manas* is the knowledge of everything that is cognised. When this knowledge and the cognised object are alike lost, there is no second path. By giving up all cognition of objects, the *manas* is absorbed and *Kaivalya* — aloneness of the Being — remains.

It will be observed that this approaches the Reality — *Sat-cit-ānanda* (Existence-consciousness-bliss) — from its *Cit* aspect, that is, as Consciousness or Knowledge.

2. Another helpful method is to begin meditation with a happy mood, with no object in view but the feeling of happiness in the heart. This can be created in so many ways in the imagination and maintained throughout the duration of meditation. Happiness, being the nature of the Self, facilitates the approach to it, provided the mind is kept easy, thought-free and alert without self-assertiveness. The mental and physical relaxation which precedes sleep is also felt here, but without its companion, torpor. This should be held on for as long a time as possible and, whenever a thought appears, it should be immediately checked to prevent a return to the welter of thinking and feeling. A conscious, thought-free and happy alertness is

the principal ingredient of this method and, when made firm by practice, it will eventually turn out to be the very consciousness of the quest. If a blank state supervenes in meditation, it should be ignored, for it will dissipate in the course of the practice, and not dwelt upon. The thought of the blank is more harmful to the meditation than the blank itself. This approaches the Reality from its *ānanda* (bliss) aspect.

3. Sri Ramana Maharshi takes the search for the root of the 'I'-sense to yield the best results, and so it has proved to many of his disciples. It is based on the undeniable fact of one's own existence, which is self-evident and, as existence is by its very definition eternal and absolute, tracing one's 'I' to its source is bound to reveal its truth. The common man identifies this 'I' with the body and becomes inextricably involved in the complex problems of the body, but the seeker has since a long time detached himself from the grossest form of this identification, as is proved by his spiritual urge. When he appears before the Guru and determines to dedicate himself to the life of the spirit, it is obvious that his 'body-I' relation has become attenuated enough to break down when persistently challenged by investigations, which, in this school, consists of the Self-inquiry 'Who am I?' The knot which ties the one to the other grows looser as the seeker's attention is more and more diverted from the insentient body to the nature of his sentient 'I'. This inquiry — *vichāra* — (which is associated with the Maharshi's name), when thoroughly

mastered and intelligently applied, acts in two ways: by meditation it wards off all other thoughts and retains the mind's purity, and by analysis and reflection it exposes the insentience and transience of the body, as contrasted with the infinite, intelligent 'I' which pervades it as life and consciousness. As the water in which a sponge has been soaked alone remains, after the sponge is removed, so does the intelligent pervader of the body alone remain when the body or body-thought is cut down by the dual process of *vichāra* and *dhyāna*. This approach to the Absolute is from the *Sat* or Being aspect.

4. There is yet another method which is used in *dhyāna* yoga by the few who cannot straightway begin meditation, namely, breath-control *(prāṇāyāma)*. A vast literature has been written on this method, with which, however, this yoga does not concern itself, except for the sole purpose of stabilising the mind. It is a proven fact that breathing and thinking function simultaneously in the waking state, so that if the breath is controlled by a special exercise, the thinking faculty follows suit as a matter of course. With alternate inhaling and exhaling, there comes in between them a short period of rest called *kumbhaka,* which secures a corresponding rest in the mind, and which by practice can be lengthened at will to bring the attention to a focus from which the *dhyāna* can start on its own. This is the strict use the *dhyāna* yogi makes of the *prāṇāyāma*. If he goes much farther than this, or fails to resort to *dhyāna*, he ceases to be a *dhyāna* yogi but a digressor into practices which lead to unpredictable ends.

The foregoing few methods of *dhyāna* are, let it be clearly understood, mere hints to the *sādhakā* to include in his own peculiar approach. Hints are also the Guru's directions. Meditation, being the spontaneous urge of the external man to surrender himself — his thoughts and feelings — to the Eternal in him, is purely individual, so that it may be truly said that meditation has as many forms as there are meditators. It may even begin with an external worship *(upāsanā)* or devotional outpourings and gradually mellows down to the point where thoughts are suspended, including that of the worshipped object, leaving the yogi's own self alone as the ultimate residue. In all cases, the external worship has eventually to turn upon itself and become Self-worship, which is the highest *bhakti (parābhakti),* than which there is no higher.

It has to be remembered that one and only one method should be used at a time, or else the yogi will be completely baffled. If he is in doubt about the advantage of his approach, he should try the one that he thinks suits him best, give it a fair trial, and then abandon it, should it prove unsuitable till he finally stumbles on the best and easiest. Generally yogis find their own form of meditation almost from the start, as naturally as free water finds its own level by an immutable natural law.

CHAPTER 4

PITFALLS

WHILE on the subject of meditation it will be worth our while to draw the attention of the *sādhakā* to the variety of sensory experiences which some beginners obtain, or imagine they obtain, in meditation. The case of the gentleman who thought he had heard an explosion inside his skull and had run out of the meditation room all atremble, is exceptional, no doubt, but by no means unique. The number of visionaries is certainly legion, but less in the ordinary state of consciousness than in meditation. Super-sensuous hearing and seeing are frequent to those who expect them and even pray for them, mistaking them for signs of Divine Grace. In this *sādhanā* they are condemned: they harass only beginners, or the mentally immature who entertain wrong, fantastic notions of the yogic practice. The world, we have seen, is but the shadow-play of the senses, to suppress which we take to *sādhanā,* so that falling victim to the senses in the very attempt at destroying them is admitting *Māyā* by the back door. Yogis must be warned against these fraudulent experiences: whatever is seen, heard, or smelt in meditation is pure fancy and, therefore, must be mercilessly ignored; it will eventually give way before a determined practice. A very large section of humanity equates miracles and visions with holiness, and the common folk in this country (India) likewise view them with undisguised awe, so that millions flock to him who can exhibit a pennyworth miracle. Vedantic India abhors them, and has a profound contempt for the conscious display of *siddhis* (psychic powers), except by the *jñāni-siddhas* on special but very infrequent occasions, for it detracts from the realisation of the Truth, which is the sole aim of this yoga. These *siddhas* must be distinguished from the so-called "Occultists", who claim to have *siddhis* but have no *Jñāna* (knowledge of the Reality), nor specifically aim at achieving it.

Those who claim and work for miracles and *siddhis*, by whatever name they are known, have no place in the path of the Absolute. The seekers of the Absolute have to guard against these lures and traps of the senses, and against the fables that circulate about the dangers of yoga. *Dhyāna* yoga must be purified from these excrescences and, being safe and simple, it can be practised by anyone, at any time, and in any healthy and clean environment and circumstance without the slightest fear or hesitation.

CHAPTER 5

SAMĀDHI

THE word *samādhi* has often been translated as "trance" in English, which is highly misleading. Trance has a bad odour, and can by no means convey the idea of *cinmātra,* the pure consciousness which is vividly experienced in the heart in *samādhi. Advaitic samādhi* has no resemblance whatever to the cataleptic trance which the mysteries of ancient Egypt and Greece were said to induce, or to the contemplation of the religious mystic. Hence I have left *samādhi* untranslated throughout this essay. The terms *Nirvāṇa* and Mind (not *manas*) used by Zen Buddhists and Mahāyānists seem to have the same connotation as *samādhi.*

Samādhi is therefore the experience of the pure, formless consciousness in the heart, which, once experienced, is never lost. The seeking will then end, and the consolidation of the experience into the permanency of *sahaja samādhi* alone remains to be achieved. With rare exceptions the early experience of *samādhi* is vague and shaky, but it acquires firmness by practice, which is no longer the same as the pre-*samādhi* practice, which has been one of searching for the Heart. Henceforth meditation is effortless to a degree, and free from the strain and doubts of the past.

If the *samādhi* continues to be disturbed by thoughts, it is called *savikalpa*, in which, though peaceful, the world, as thoughts, is still feebly present. It has not yet become firm enough to free itself from thinking, which is the characteristic of the next higher *samādhi*, the *nirvikalpa*, wherein the mind stands poised in the stillness of the Heart. This is the *Svarūpa* (the very nature) of existence and of all things, the Being or Self absolute. When by constant practice *nirvikalpa samādhi* is turned into *sahaja,* Self-realisation or *Jīvanmukti* — the state of Liberation-in-life — is said to have been achieved. The *Jīvanmukta* is permanently aware of his reality as consciousness-bliss.

I have given these details in the hope of dispelling some of the myths which have been woven by imaginative writers round *nirvikalpa* and around *samādhi*. The mysteries which are said to shroud them do not exist at all. *Samādhi* is the state of one's own true Self, in which all human endeavours find fulfilment. Love for power, wealth, fame, country, service of humanity or religious worship has *samādhi*, or Self-discovery, alone for its objective. For him who has achieved it there remains nothing more to do or aspire for in life: he has realised his own truth, as the all, the soul of all, dwelling ever and ever in the hearts of all. And because his state is beyond common experience, it has been subject to so much speculation and unintelligent guess-work. Hence is the need for the above details.

CHAPTER 6

THE SĀTTVIC FOOD

IN every country in this wide world there are a good number of people who lead a virtuous life and attempt to tread the path of true religion and piety, each according to his light. Of these not a few aspire to follow the Vedantic tradition, and are eager to know the kind of diet they should adopt for this purpose. Their eagerness is quite understandable, considering the distinct effects of food and drink on our physical and moral well-being — effects which can be by no means minimised. Who has not been a witness to the injuries of strong liquor to oneself and one's near and dear, or to the suffering caused by certain articles of diet to a constitution which is not suited to them? And when the body is struck down by a disease, or becomes upset, the mind, which is our most precious asset, goes down the same slope. This is what caused the ancients to prescribe a regimen for the yogi and warn him against indiscriminate feeding.

To perform *sādhanā* a sound health is of paramount importance. We cannot be too careful to avoid anything which is likely to disturb the balance of our physical economy. The quantity of food we ingest is not of less importance than its quality. And no food can be expected to yield the desired nourishment but the simplest, which is easily digestible, prevents accumulation, fermentation and general discomfort. This food we call *sāttvic* (harmonious, compatible, agreeable) and is of much help to the *sādhanā*. No hard and fast rule can be made for the articles which should be used in the diet. Constitutions differ; so do climatic conditions. What is good for one person and in one part of the world may not be good for another and in another part of the world. The question of availability must be also considered. Yet so much can be said about the diet in general, namely, that animal food is discouraged in this path, especially if the animal concerned is developed in bulk, or low and loathsome in habits. One need hardly specify. He who has chosen this spiritual line will not fail to distinguish between the clean and the unclean, and between what is good for him to eat and what is not.

In India the food served in ashrams and temples as well as in most brahmin houses consists of some of the following: rice, wheat, pulses, milk, butter, ghee, fresh vegetables, nuts, etc., cooked in simple style, in addition to fruits and moderate quantities of tea and coffee. There are also very large non-Brahmin communities all over the country which consider it a sacrilege to feed on flesh, so that a very high percentage of the Hindu population is pure vegeterian and, notwithstanding, keeps a robust health and sturdy constitution. As for drink, nothing can be healthier than pure, fresh water. Intoxicants are strictly prohibited; for they fuddle and muddy up the mind which with extreme care we are preparing for the supreme experience. It is only when the body is healthy and in perfect ease, and the mind clear, happy and alert that this yoga can succeed.

> Yoga killeth all pain for him who is regulated in eating and leisure, regulated in working, regulated in sleeping and waking. When his subdued mind is fixed in the Self, free from longing for desirable objects, then he is said to be harmonised.
>
> (*Bhagavad Gītā,* VI, 17, 18)

CHAPTER 7

SĀDHAKĀS (PRACTISING DISCIPLES)

TRUTH seekers who resort to a *Brahmarṣi* (the Sage who has realised Brahman, the Absolute or Self) for guidance are of great variety. They are not and cannot all be of the same mental and spiritual outlook, the same intellectual abilities or constitutional make up, to follow the same course of meditation, or hold to it for the same length of time, etc. Modes of meditation differ from one *sādhaka* to another, as modes of thinking and of self-expression differ among individuals in ordinary life. Inspirations and light come to all of them in various ways, and each follows them as best suits his temperament and in the manner most conducive to his progress. Again, not all come with the same amount of preparation to their credit. Some are ripe, some less so, others are people of the world with yet very strong inclinations for the life spiritual. Some begin with material motives but get caught on the way and turn spiritual.

The Guru knows each and every one of them, yet keeps his own counsel. In his infinite compassion he looks upon all with an eye of perfect equality, so that each disciple may, in his free and pure atmosphere, rise to the greatest heights of his spiritual potentialities. Grace and holiness flow from the Guru as spontaneously as light flows from the sun, or fragrance from the flower. They are ceaseless and infinite.

The foremost *sādhakā* is he who has surrendered himself completely to the practice, which he views as the only reason for his being in an embodied existence. Nothing else matters to him. His mind remains fixed on the search for the Heart, whether in his meditation, which is the time for intense concentration, or in his studies. In this mood he makes rapid progress, for then the mind will be able to shed quickly much of its inherited encumbrances and propensities — its *vāsanās* — and replace them by the habits of the quest. He asks nothing of the Guru that has no bearing on his *sādhanā*, and desires nothing but to be left in peace to pursue it in his own way.

Next is the *sādhakā* who cannot sustain a prolonged concentration, but compensates himself by long stays in the presence of the Guru and more study. After him comes the one who cannot meditate at all, preferring to serve the Guru in all sorts of ways. He earns the merit of serving a Guru and a *Brahmarṣi* and at the same time benefits by his tranquil atmosphere, with the result that his mind will, in course of time, be fit for meditation.

Next is the devotee who does not strictly come in the *sādhakā* category. He does not stay with the Guru, but visits him off and on, and performs *sādhanā* in his own way at home. He may have a family whom he finds it his duty to maintain and look after. There is no valid objection to a married life, notwithstanding the widespread prejudice against it. The objection is to the net of complexities which a married life, especially in the present-day society, weaves round the life of the seeker, which impels many of them to keep away from matrimonial ties in order to be free to surrender themselves to the life contemplative.

Many other classes of devotees crowd round the Guru, ranging from the householder who considers *sādhanā* superfluous, taking the Master to be like a solid raft which carries all the passenger-devotees to the other shore of *mukti* (Liberation) with all their luggage of sins and shortcomings, to the one who expects a return on his devotion, or the one who first puts the Guru to the test in his worldly affairs before accepting him. All these benefit by their attachment to the Master, for no one who draws near the fire will miss being comforted to a degree by its warmth. The Guru, like the sun, sheds his light on one and all, leaving it to each devotee to receive the quantum which is commensurate with his ability to absorb. Worldliness sticks to all the disciples in various degrees, which the Master's holy presence mysteriously rubs off, particularly in those who cooperate in their *sādhanā* with humility, detachment, and a strong commonsense.

The variety of ways God or the Self brings men to him is amazing to watch. No one is forgotten; no one is for ever left behind, and no one is totally annihilated as a 'lost soul' for whatever wickedness one has at one time or other been guilty of. The creed of lost souls is not that of the Vedanta: it does not fit in with its teaching of the single Substance, single Existence.

CHAPTER 8

CONCLUSION

THOSE who are already *sādhakās* are on the highway to Release. To them there is nothing more to say. They are already safe. Nor is there anything more to say to those who are on the brink. These need a little push — a gentle push — and they will be soon squatting at the feet of the Guru, appealing for light. The more sluggish ones need a more forcible push to make them fall into line with the former. To these one would suggest: do not lag behind and waste your time in useless things. Do not wait for the knock down. You are almost a renouncer. Start your march towards your destined goal right now, as start you will some day, somehow. Change your outlook on life and your values of the things in which you have reposed your trust for happiness. For none can give you true happiness, neither man, woman nor even God Himself, but the spiritual strength derived from self-restraint, self-discovery, and aspirations for Truth.

Kaivalya Upaniṣad begins with a prayer of the disciple to Lord Parameṣṭi, the Supreme Guru:

O Lord pray impart to me the most excellent wisdom *(Brahmavidyā)*, which is ever enjoyed by the

Enlightened Ones, and by which, the wise, having freed themselves from all sins, reach Puruṣa, the Most High.

The Blessed Lord answers:

Know it thou through Faith, Devotion, Meditation, and through Yoga. For neither by action (ritualistic) nor by progeny or wealth is Liberation attained, but by Renunciation alone.

*Paramahamsas** of pure mind, by realising the true meaning of the highest Vedanta through the Yoga of Renunciation (Sannyāsa Yoga) enter into That, which is above Heaven and which resides in the Cave of the Heart, and thus attain Liberation.

---

* *Paramahamsas* are the yogis who follow the path of Direct Liberation in this life. (See Preface and *Nāradaparivrājaka Upaniṣad*)

BOOK II

MĀṆḌŪKYOPANIṢAD

INTRODUCTORY

THE importance of this midget Upaniṣad can be judged by the evidence of the *Muktikopaniṣad* which says that "The only means by which final Emancipation is obtained is through the *Māṇḍūkya Upaniṣad* alone, which is enough for the salvation of all aspirants."

Besides, it is not for nothing that Gauḍapāda chose it from all the major Upaniṣads to write his ponderous *Kārikās* on. It offers the briefest, clearest, and most practical study of the nature of man, or *Ātman* (Self), which it equates with the absolute Reality.

Whilst it does not explain how to realise it, by its exposition of the three strata of consciousness and the one *Ātman* prevailing in all of them, the Yogi will not fail, through long-continued practice, to sense and finally realise it as his own very self, ever perfect, changeless and eternal in the Fourth *(Turīya)* State generally known as *samādhi*.

Suggestiveness is the very essence of this Upaniṣad, so that he who is endowed with a quick perception will make the most rapid progress in the shortest time he is capable of.

The notes written after each *Śruti* are a small attempt to bring out in the modern language to the modern seeker, who abhors long pedantic quotations and abstruse explanations, its most salient points. But they can by no means take the place of the compendious commentaries written on them by the illustrious Masters Gauḍapāda and Śaṅkara. Readers who wish to extend their knowledge of this great Upaniṣad will do well to make a deep study of these immortal contributions.

Shruti 1

HARi AUM = The one principle that does not change. Endures & transcends all.

The Supreme BRAHMAN

= Absolute Reality. = Answers all questions

= Lord Vishnu. = Resolves all doubt

= Pure Consciousness

= CiT. = ananda

= The Knower & the Known.

AUM ⇒ The being of the Self

Waking State (JAGRAT)

The JiVA (individual)

VISVA (Vaisvanara)

DREAMING State (SVApana)

The individual JiVA

TAiJasa

Dreamless sleep (Susupti) State

Jiva

PRAJna

TURiya

When the JiVA realizes himself as the absolute Atman ⇒ Devoid of all objective experiences but includes them all.

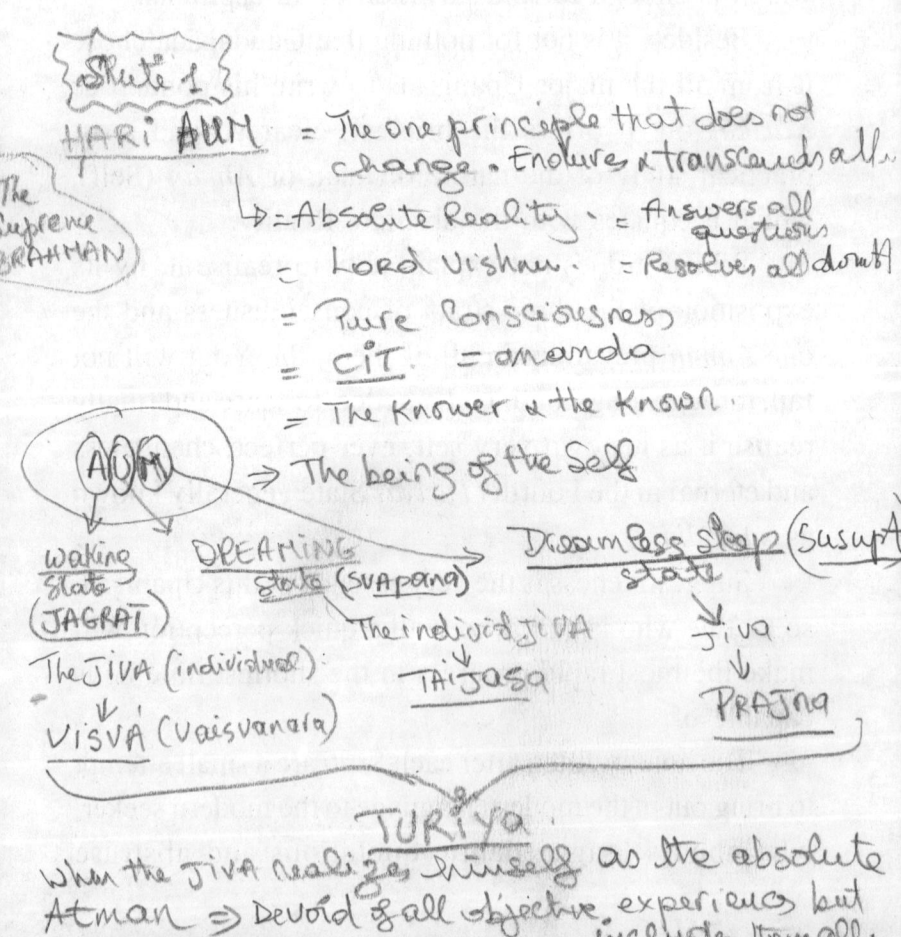

THE MĀṆḌŪKYOPANIṢAD

VEDIC INVOCATION

May our ears, O Devas, hear (only) auspicious sounds, our eyes see (only) auspicious forms. May we, your beloved, in healthy bodies with sound limbs, enjoy our allotted years, full of the praise of the Most High. Aum Peace! Peace!! Peace!!!

Śruti I

Hariḥ Aum. The word Aum is all this — a clear explanation follows. All that is past, present and future is truly Aum. So is also Aum that which lies beyond the triple concept of time.

Note: The Māṇḍūkya, it will be observed, does not waste words: it takes for granted that the reader has already studied much and has long reflected on a world which he does not fully comprehend — a world of ceaseless change, of uncertainties, of lack of logical sequence, of senseless inequalities, of birth, growth, decay and death, of afflictions and tribulations of all kinds, which pain, puzzle and confuse him.

So from the very start it plunges into the heart of the quest and points out the one principle which does not change, which endures through and transcends all change. This is the absolute Reality, the realisation of which answers all questions and resolves all doubts. This principle the *Māṇḍūkya* calls the word 'Aum'.

This *Śruti* has earned for itself the reputation of being a hard nut to crack. Let us examine it closely to see how 'the explanation' justifies this epithet and the foregoing conclusion.

'Hariḥ Aum' which begins it makes it clear that Aum is not other than Hari, Lord Viṣṇu, whose nature is pure Consciousness *(Cit)*, absolute Knowledge. As the one and only Knower, He is the changeless unity underlying all He knows, namely, 'all this', i.e. the changing world of diversity which it also includes in Aum. Thus Aum is the knower and Aum the known, because the knower knows only his thoughts, which emanate from, and are, thus, of the same substance as, him. The diversity, therefore, although included in Aum, is not actual but ideal, existing only in the consciousness. And, to corroborate this ideality of the diversity, the *Śruti* includes also in Aum 'all that is past, present, and future', turning the diversity into a mere experience, a mere thought, again, in the experiencer (Hari, *Ātman* or Self; see next *Śruti*), for time makes sense only in terms of the experience.

Read as a whole, therefore, this *Śruti* obviously implies that man the experiencer (Ātman) alone is real, that is, he alone exists, either as the changing phenomena (or thought) or as their changeless substratum, the Self, which transcends time, like gold which remains gold whether perceived as metal, or in a variety of shapes as ornaments. Hence whatever and wherever we see, outwardly or inwardly, either in the world of sense or in the world of pure thought, it is the one Self, man as he is in himself, alone, we see and nought else.

The uniqueness of the *Māṇḍūkya Upaniṣad* consists in its proving the existence of the Self in all states and conditions as their experiencer by making each letter of Aum to stand for it in each of the three states of consciousness, as the waker, dreamer and sleeper. The experiencer of the Fourth *(Turīya)* is symbolised by joining all the three letters together to make the word 'Aum'. So the Self in *Turīya* is the experiencer of all the three other states as Aum includes all its three letters.

In the waking state *(jāgrat)*, when the senses are fully awake and perceive a world which the *jīva* (the individual) believes to be real, he takes the name of *Vaiśvānara,* or simply *Viśva,* as represented by the letter A. When Viśva withdraws his senses into himself and takes to dreaming, his name becomes *Taijasa,* corresponding to the letter U. Abandoning even the dream state *(svapna)* and remaining in the aloneness *(kaivalya)* of his own Self, he is then said to be in dreamless sleep *(suṣupti)*, when he takes the name of *Prājña,* represented by the letter M. But when, after full maturity *(adhikāra)* in *jāgrat,* he realises himself as the absolute *Ātman*, his name becomes *Turīya,* who is devoid of all objective experiences but includes them all, as the word Aum includes all its letters. Thus Aum is the being of Self undergoing all the experiences of all the states: those which lie within the triple series of time, namely, *jāgrat* and *svapna,* and those which lie beyond time, namely, *suṣupti* and *Turīya,* of which more is discussed in the following *śrutis*.

The two words 'Hariḥ Aum', referred to above, with which this *śruti* commences actually sum up, at the very outset, not only the whole *śruti*, but the whole Māṇḍūkya. Hari, the Supreme Brahman, whose nature is pure Consciousness *(cit)* and bliss *(ānanda),* is equated with Aum, which is equated with 'all this', making everything to be constituted of nothing but of pure Consciousness. This, in fact, is the quintessence of the whole Upaniṣadic lore.

Śruti II

> All this is truly *Brahman*: this (Self) is *Brahman*: it has four *pādās*.

Note: *Brahman* is the infinite Consciousness, absolute Knowledge. Thus 'All this,' '*Ātman*,' '*Brahman,*' 'Aum' are the one and same Reality. The literal meaning of *pādās* is feet, but Śaṅkara translates it as quarters. However, both the translations seem equally to serve the purpose of this *śruti*, which aims at determining the number of the states through which *Ātman*, man the real, has to pass. But Śaṅkara's interpretation seems to imply that the subject's perfection can be achieved only if all the four states of consciousness are experienced, or else it would remain incomplete, as the unit remains incomplete if all its four quarters are not integrated in it. This translation seems to compel the inclusion of *Turīya* into the number of the states to achieve the desired goal of Liberation. For the whole humanity daily passes through the three states mentioned before, but *Turīya* none can experience but the yogi through intense preparations and spiritual practices.

It is evident that according to the Māṇḍūkya, apart from these four states, there exists no other state or world for man to experience, either before or after "death": neither heaven nor hell, nor any other known or unknown plane of existence. If any does exist it should only be dream-like; for the senses, which create objective experience, i.e., a world, can function only in a physical body, which contains the necessary instruments, like so many transistors, through which they can manifest themselves, namely, the sensory organs. But a physical body is obtainable only on this "earth", i.e., in the waking state. Therefore, there can be no other states than those of which this Upaniṣad speaks. This is the second main point of the Māṇḍūkya, the first being the presence of the Self at all times and in all places, in all states and conditions, as explained above as the ALL.

Śruti III

The first *pāda* is *Vaiśvānara*, whose field is *jāgrat*. He is conscious of external objects and possesses seven limbs and nineteen mouths, and has gross objects for experience.

Note: That *Viśva* is the first quarter of Aum has already been explained, but the fact must be again stressed that the Self is indivisible and has no parts to be divided into halves and quarters. The quarters here mentioned are mere conventional names given to the same being as he experiences the different states of consciousness, as symbolised by the different letters of AUM. *Viśva* stands first in the enumeration because he has a physical body to experience the waking state, which supplies the impressions upon which the dream state stands and also because he is then all-knowing. He empirically knows what dreams are, what deep sleep means, and also the existence of such a state as *samādhi* or *Turīya,* although he may not know their real nature. But as *Taijasa* and *Prājña* he does not know *jāgrat* although in *jāgrat* he knows them both; for in *jāgrat* all his faculties (or senses) are awake and active, whereas in dreams they are mere shadows of their *jāgrat* selves.

"He is conscious of external objects" (in *jāgrat*) is due to the presence of these faculties, which force on his attention an external world, which is actually his own internal thoughts. Objects, space, time, movements, memories are illusions foisted by the senses on him. Memory is the most formidable of them, for it perpetuates in his consciousness most of his experiences, gives rise to the sense of 'I' and 'mine', the sense of relationships, of cause and effect, etc., etc.

Yet *jāgrat* is not without its merits in that it eventually compels *Viśva*, through long series of painful experiences, to break the chain of his slavery to the world phenomena and be free to cognise himself as he is by nature, *which in no other state is possible.* It is only in a physical body that he can perceive, think, reflect, perform *tapas* (austerities), and receive his reward in *Turīya,* which is the blissful Liberation.

The seven limbs and nineteen mouths are Viśva's instruments of knowledge and action *(Jñānendriyās* and *karmendriyās* respectively) lodged in the body (of which Srī Śaṅkara gives a detailed account in his commentary on this *śloka*) through which the senses reveal their powers.

Śruti IV

> *Taijasa* is the second *pāda* and his field consists of dreams, when he is conscious of internal objects, has seven limbs and nineteen mouths, and experiences subtle objects.

.*Note:* We have already seen that the man of the Self takes the name of *Taijasa* when he passes on to the dream state *(svapna)*, corresponding to the letter U of Aum after having been *Viśva* in the waking. The study of this state helps us to understand the true nature of the waking world by an analogy which has no parallel.

Everyone dreams and knows that dreams are empty of substance, being mere fancy of the dreaming mind. The same may be said of the waking — the creation of *Viśva's* mind. All objects, all movements, ideas, sensations or actions of the waking have no real substance or existence independent of the mind in which they take place.

Śrutis III and IV speak of the subject in *jāgrat* perceiving external objects, whereas in dreams he perceives internal objects. The fact is in dreams also he perceives external space and thinks he is in contact with external objects as he does in *jāgrat*. It is only after coming out of the dream to the waking state that he realises that what he had taken to be outside was only inside him. In *jāgrat* also he imagines the objects to be outside but they prove to be inside him when he steps out of *jāgrat* into *Turīya* (or *samādhi)*.

The "subtle objects" which *Taijasa* experiences are the impressions he carries from *jāgrat:* a doctor, for example, dreams of medicines and patients; an air pilot of engines and flying; a mathematician tries to solve his unsolved equations, and so on. But the *Jīvanmukta* who is in permanent *Turīya*, experiences vague, shapeless dreams, because his *jāgrat* impressions are too weak to create bold, well-formed dreams. His mind has become so attenuated that objects leave hardly any mark on it in *jāgrat* to be projected to the dream state.

Śruti V

Dreamless sleep is that state in which the sleeper desires no object nor sees any dream. *Prājña* is the third *pāda* and his field is deep sleep, wherein the whole becomes one, undifferentiated. He is truly a mass of consciousness, full of bliss and experiences bliss and is the gateway to knowledge.

Note: This *(suṣupti)* is the most instructive of the three common states, for from it we infer the independence of the soul from the body, its survival of death, and its eternal freedom. Bondage results from the perception and acquisition of desirable objects. In dreamless sleep the subject is devoid of bodies and perception, and thus of bondage and misery. He is then sunk in the bliss of *kaivalya* (the aloneness of the pure being). The inference is that the body is not the man, nor is it necessary for his existence. That being the case, death loses its sting, and the fear of total annihilation becomes a mockery.

In deep sleep the subject takes the name of *Prājña,* corresponding to the letter M (of Aum). All his experiences — internal and external — as well as all his possessions as *Viśva* and *Taijasa* — body, name, fame, human relationships, position, fortune and misfortunes, health and diseases, etc., etc., of the waking and dream states merge then into him and become 'one, undifferentiated' mass. The multiplicity then becomes a unity. He is then neither man, woman, nor child; neither human nor non-human. The *jāgrat* king is then no king, nor the *jāgrat* beggar beggar, the murderer is no murderer, nor the saint saint, even the worm becomes then the one being, which is a 'mass of consciousness and bliss'.

He is *Prājña,* 'the gateway to knowledge' because he is the source and container of the faculties which create the other two states of objective perception as well as the faculty which cognises the Self in the state of *Turīya*.

The word 'sleeper' implies that *Prājña* is unaware of his own being. He is likewise unaware of its bliss. Therefore, 'he experiences bliss' simply means that he is actually in bliss but is not at the moment aware of it: he acknowledges it on his return to *jāgrat,* when his memory and intellect revive and reminisce the 'refreshing', 'sound' sleep. In *Turīya* alone he becomes aware of the bliss, as he does of the Self. Again this word ('sleeper') does not mean that *Prājña* actually sleeps, for the Self is changeless, neither wakes nor sleeps. He is called sleeper only in *jāgrat,* contrasting him to himself as *Viśva* and *Taijasa*.

Śruti VI

> This is the Lord of all, the knower of all, the inner controller, the source from which all things originate and into which they finally dissolve.

Note: This *śruti* develops the points of the previous one to stress once again the eternal truth that man by nature is pure spirit, pure knowledge and bliss ever free from body and mind, which (in *jāgrat*) distract his attention from the singleness of his self to a false sense of diversity, tempting him to desire and act, and then suffer the consequences.

"This is the Lord of all," because when as *Viśva* he projects the senses and creates an imaginary world from himself, he unknowingly becomes the "all", which he cognises and enjoys as its lord. Being the source of the senses which he can withdraw or project at will, he is said to be their inner controller as well as their final receptacle when they slip back again in him, the changeless Brahman. He is, again, the "inner controller" when he acts as life and controls the function of every organ in the body, making the body move, think, and speak as if it were the man himself.

Śruti VII

> *Turīya* is not he who is conscious of the internal world, nor he who is conscious of the external, nor he who is conscious of both, nor he who is a mass of sentience, nor he who is simple consciousness, nor he who is insentient. (He is) unseen, unrelated, incomprehensible, uninferable, inconceivable, indescribable, of the nature of consciousness in essence and constitutes the Self alone, totally devoid of phenomena, all peace and bliss, and non-dual. This is known as *Turīya:* it is the Self and has to be realised.

Note: We now come to the object of the quest, the immediate apprehension of the Supreme Self in the state known as *Turīya,* the Fourth. But first we have to note that *Turīya* is the name given not only to the fourth quarter of *Ātman*, the experiencer of the fourth state, but also to the fourth state itself, unlike the other states which have their own names as different from the names of their experiencer, for in it the object is the subject himself, the cognised state is the cogniser's own self — "I am this."

The first part of this *śruti* obviously refers to the three common *pādās* of Aum — *Viśva, Taijasa* and *Prājña* — from whom *Turīya* differs in his having none of their experiences. By "simple consciousness" is meant *siddhis* — omniscience, prophetic visions and the like, which are also thoughts, covering the perception of the Self.

The epithets "unseen, unrelated, uninferable," etc., referring to *Turīya* are meant as a warning to the reader against forming a conception of it other than being of the "nature of consciousness, totally devoid of phenomena, all-bliss and non-dual." *Sādhakas* in particular are prone to such preconceptions, which later experience proves to be erroneous. The *Mahāvākya* (the great scriptural dictum) "I am Brahman" and the like, which are sometimes prescribed for meditation, do not describe *Turīya,* but stress the reality, eternity and freedom of the being, the meditator's own Self.

Turīya is not a "mass of sentience" distinguishes him from *Prājña,* in whom "the whole becomes one, undifferentiated" without the slightest tinge of insentience — perception, thought or action. Whereas in *Turīya* the senses and the faculties of cognition are all present but subdued to be conscious of the state, which is "the Self alone", "of the nature of consciousness in essence." The *śruti* thus enjoins us not to conceive, portray, or infer *Turīya,* but to wait till we experience it, as experience it we must, some day, for it is the inevitable goal of mankind.

Śruti VIII

The same *Ātman* is also Aum as viewed as a syllable, also Aum with parts as viewed as sound. The *pādas* are the letters — A, U and M — and the letters the *pādas* (quarters).

Note: The Māṇḍūkya has so far dealt with Aum as synonymous with *Ātman* as Consciousness, passing through the four states as its four quarters. Here it points out their physical resemblance first as a unit and then as sound. *Ātman* is as single as Aum, because the latter consists of one single syllable. Their resemblance as sound is denoted by the different sounds of the different letters of Aum, each of which stands for the Self, (*Ātman*) as *Viśva, Taijasa* and *Prājña*.

We have now to conclude that all this emphasis by the Māṇḍūkya on the identity of *Ātman* with Aum has the one purpose of proving that man in himself is the one changeless reality, ever existent, ever the same, though he appears to wake, dream and sleep; that the body and the world are nought but thoughts superimposed on him; and that he is bound to realise them as such in the state known as the Fourth, which is not other than his own true nature.

Śruti IX

Vaiśvānara, who has the waking state for his field, is A, the first letter, because he is all-pervading, or his being the first. He who knows this will have all his desires fulfilled and becomes the first.

Note: *Śruti* III has already dealt with *Viśva*. His resemblance to A consists first in the fact that he pervades the whole universe, in thought, as its knower (in the waking state), just as the sound A pervades all the sounds of the other letters of the alphabet, and, secondly, that *Viśva* is the experiencer of the first of the states through which *Ātman* passes, just as A, being the first letter of the alphabet, pervades the whole alphabet.

Śruti X

Taijasa, who has the dream state for his field, is U, the second letter, because he is superior, or because he stands between the two. He attains to superior knowledge who knows this, is treated by all equally, and will have no one in his posterity who is not a knower of Brahman.

Note: The dreamer is considered superior to the waker on account of his being divested of the senses which overwhelm the latter with the potent illusions they create and also on account of his being nearer to the blissful *kaivalya* which prevails in *suṣupti*. The knower of this truth is evidently spiritually superior to the man who is totally ignorant of it, for he is a seeker and fast moving towards the realisation of it in *Turīya*.

The resemblance of *Taijasa* to the letter U of Aum consists in the fact that he comes between *Viśva* and *Prājña,* swimming so to say, between the shores of *jāgrat* and those of *suṣupti,* as the U stands between A and M. "He is treated by all equally," because he treats all equally, as the Supreme Brahman.

Śruti XI

> *Prājña*, who has sleep for his field, is M, the third letter of Aum, because he is the measure and in whom all become one. He who knows this can measure and understand all things within himself.

Note: The Self which experiences deep sleep, stands by himself, free from the superimpositions which afflict him when he functions as *Viśva* and *Taijasa*. He is then pure Being, that is, the same in all sentient beings, where distinction between humans and non-humans does not exist. Being not one of nature but only of outer manifestation, the diversity perceived by *Viśva* and *Taijasa* melts into the unity of being in *Prājña* and re-awakes when *Prājña* "re-awakes" once again as *Viśva* and *Taijasa*. Hence *Prājña* is the measure of all. His resemblance to M consists in his absorbing *Viśva* and *Taijasa* in sleep as the sound of M absorbs the sounds of A and U when the word is uttered. The knower of this is evidently the knower of the true nature of things.

Śruti XII

> *Turīya*, who has no parts (as sound), who is incomprehensible, the cessation of all phenomena, the blissful and non-dual Aum, is truly identical with *Ātman*. He who knows this merges into the *Ātman*.

Note: This *śruti* does not compare *Ātman* with the letters of Aum, for in *Turīya* the other three *Viśva, Taijasa* and *Prājña* — integrate, as all the letters of Aum integrate in the word Aum. As *Turīya*, the yogi enters into the full realisation of himself as that pure, non-dual, changeless *Ātman* which has never been other than itself, though it appeared to have passed through the triple experience of the other three states, which have now proved to be nothing but dream-like movements within itself, movements which have now come to an absolute end. He further realises the full import of the *Mahāvākya* 'I am Brahman' in his complete identity with it. For *knowing* the *Ātman* is *being* the *Ātman*.

BOOK III

ĀTMA BODHA
OF
ŚRĪ ŚAṄKARĀCĀRYA

INTRODUCTORY

ĀTMA BODHA is one of the smallest treatises written by Ācārya Śaṅkara, but it occupies a unique place in the science of Self-knowledge and Liberation, which, evidently, makes it the favourite of yogis and truth-seekers. In sixty-eight short stanzas the celebrated author gives the cream of the *Vedānta* — the ultimate truth, the nature of Existence, the relation of man to it on the one hand and to the world on the other, the primal ignorance *(avidyā)* with which he is afflicted and which keeps him tied to the wheel of birth and death, pleasure and pain and, finally, the method by which he can liberate himself from it and attain the bliss of absolute knowledge, which is also absolute truth.

As nothing but light can dispel darkness, the great Ācārya asserts, nothing but knowledge can dispel ignorance. Not action and ritualistic worship, but fervent desire for release can induce reflection and investigation, which ultimately liberate.

Although Brahman, the Absolute, is said to be undefinable because it is unconditioned by attributes which can be conceived from sense impressions, Śaṅkara gives an idea of it as the consciousness which cognises the impressions. Impressions are mere thoughts (or sensations) having varieties of qualities, some gross, some fine, some finer, etc.: they rise from the thinker, the cognising consciousness, ceaselessly change, and finally subside in the thinker which is one and changeless. The changes are, therefore, not in the thinker, the consciousness (or Brahman), but in its thoughts, which are its objects, itself being the fixed, so to say, subject, so that to arrive at it, the yogi has to divest himself of all his thoughts, when the cognising mind, remaining alone, may cognise itself as the eternal source of all thoughts and sensations of the external as well as the internal world. The subject and the object, the emanator and the emanation, thus become one and the same reality.

This is the Supreme Knowledge which Śaṅkara proclaims to infallibly annihilate ignorance.

Ātma Bodha aims, therefore, at liberating the seeker from his bondage through ceaseless practice (stanza 5), for which he has to renounce all action (stanza 68). He will then attain immortality, freedom from birth and death, and everlasting felicity.

It is to be hoped that the brief, unsophisticated commentaries made on the stanzas will benefit those to whom this subject is new and who intend to tread the arduous path with fervour and determination.

ĀTMA BODHA

1. This treatise on the knowledge of the Self is being enunciated for the benefit of those who have purified themselves by penance, who are of calm mind, free from cravings, and aspire for Liberation.

Note: Before beginning to impart the supreme Knowledge that leads to Liberation, which is the aim and object of this short treatise, the author warns the reader that he is not approaching a subject which anyone can imagine himself qualified to understand. No one is so qualified, he insists, but him who has purified his mind from age-long propensities *(vāsanās)* and attachment to sense-objects and has prepared it to receive the absolute Truth. It is evident that beginners cannot presume to comprehend his ideas in the spirit with which he makes them from the first or second reading, still less to assimilate them. For if the mind has not attained that high intuitive subtlety, which results from assiduous practice and reflection, it will not only remain in a state of opacity, or semi-opacity, when it listens to these stanzas, but will in no time forget even the little grasp it has made of them. Having no foothold in experience, nor previous impressions of their profound import, through study and meditation, this little grasp will quickly slip away from the memory. Hence Śaṅkara deems it imperative to warn the reader at the outset not to be misled by the apparent simplicity of his enunciation, but to endeavour to rise to the requisite level of consciousness through mental purification, quiescence, and constant aspirations in order to reach its innermost meaning.

> 2. Of all the means to Liberation, Knowledge is the most direct one, like fire which is the most direct means of cooking. Without knowledge no emancipation is possible.

Note: Having described the qualified student to receive this teaching, the *Ācārya* turns to settle a point which from time immemorial exercised the minds of the pandits and induced hot controversies in their debates, each party claiming strong supports in the *Bhagavad Gītā*. It is the question of whether *karma* (dedicated action, or ritualistic worship), *bhakti* (devotion) or *jñāna* (knowledge or Self-realisation) is the most direct means to Liberation. He forthrightly declares in favour of the last and proceeds to give his reasons.

> 3. Karma cannot destroy ignorance, for it is not hostile to it. Knowledge alone destroys it, as light destroys darkness.

Note: "Action (karma) cannot destroy ignorance" because it is created, supported and perpetuated by ignorance. We act because we perceive gross objects, conceive a desire for them, and strive to obtain them, which very often results in suffering. We do not foresee the suffering because of the impetuosity of our passion which blinds us to the real nature of the desired objects and to the consequences of acquiring them. Action, therefore, promotes rather than destroys ignorance like the darkness that is added to darkness. That is why the Scriptures recommend renunciation of action for the attainment of Liberation.

As for desireless action *(niṣkāma karma),* it is, like ritualistic worship, also devoid of knowledge, but it is recommended to purify the mind and make it fit for the prescribed discipline of *vichāra* (enquiry) and *dhyāna* (meditation), which is the path of knowledge proper. *Yoga Vāṣiṣṭha* says, "Perfection is attained only by knowing the transcendent Spirit, and not by austerities and religious practices... Austerities, charity, vows are of no value whatever: it is by knowing one's nature that God is known." (III, vi, 164).

4. The Self appears finite through ignorance. On the removal of ignorance, the infinite Self will, of itself, stand revealed, as does the sun on the dispersal of the clouds.

Note: The one and only theme of this treatise is knowledge of the Self, with which the first stanza opens. Because there is ignorance of the Self, man's own true nature, there is ignorance of all other things. Hence the author speaks of the need of the removal of ignorance, so that the Self may reveal itself by its own light, like the cloudless sun which stands self revealed. (stanza 29).

The question now arises to whom does the infinite Self "appear finite," i.e. to whom is the ignorance? Certainly not to the Self which is pure light, pure knowledge, but to the Self which has taken a body and has become an individual (*jīva*), losing its Self-knowledge. To recover this knowledge the following practice is prescribed.

5. By ceaseless practice knowledge purifies the *jīva* from its ignorance and then itself disappears, like the *kataka* powder after cleansing the water.

Note: Here then is the method of destroying *avidyā* (ignorance): constant practice of the means of knowledge — study, reflection, meditation, ratiocination — will not fail eventually to climinate ignorance. Zen Buddhism, like Advaitism, takes its stand on the obvious fact that the mind, being the repository of both knowledge and ignorance, the medium of all sensible and supersensible experiences, alone must be enquired into to arrive at the truth about the (experienced) phenomena as well as the (experiencing) mind itself. Eventually the former will prove to be not other than the modification of the latter, its waves, so to say. Hence Zen calls Mind (with Capital M) what we generally call Self, that is, the mind as it is by itself, and mind (*manas*, with small m) when it is preoccupied with or covered by these — its waves. The practice of spiritual discipline *(sādhanā)* diverts the mind from the phenomena and turns it upon itself, so that from being the ever-disturbed, *avidyā*-covered, fear- and vice-ridden finite mind, it may become the quiescent, pure, infinite Mind, when the *sādhanā* comes to an end, like the *kataka* powder which sinks after cleansing the water of its mud.

The *jīva* of the text is the empirical man (mentioned in the last Note) who has to shed his false identification with the body to realise himself as the absolute Brahman. In common parlance it is called "ego." Some theorists put forward the argument that the mind, if cognised by itself, becomes an object to a subject, which defeats, they say, the claim of non-dual, ultimate truth for it. They seem to forget that the mind is not a gross object, say, a piece of wood, but always a knower, so that by cognising itself it does not cease to be the cognising subject also. This objectivity is not the common objectivity in which the object is, unlike the subject, insentient, but the identity of both. Moreover, in this yogic state the mind rests in itself *(samādhi)* and the notion of subject and object entirely vanishes (stanza 41), or else Self-realisation would be a conceptual jargon rather than the living experience that it is. Again, stanzas 4 and 29 compare the Self to the sun which reveals itself without the aid of another sun; categorically negating the duality of subject and object in the Supreme Consciousness.

6. Replete with affections and aversions this world (of transmigration), like a dream, appears as real while it lasts, but proves unreal on waking.

7. So long as Brahman, the substratum of all, the one without a second, is not known, the world seems real, like silver in mother-of-pearl.

Note: Description of the world begins. Śaṅkara compares this world of opposite experiences — pleasure and pain, love and hate, life and death, hunger and repletion — to a dream. All of us dream and know that dreams are mere dramatisation by the mind of a world that has no basis in reality, although at the time it appears to be real, possessing its own natural laws, time and space, cause and effect, etc. The dream is produced by the mind, and enacted by the mind upon the ground of the mind, so that there exists nothing but mind in it — itself the actor, itself the acted, and itself the acted upon or substratum. This waking state is just another such dream, superimposed by the consciousness upon the same consciousness. Due to the awakened senses it assumes a strong appearance of reality and induces us to work with the view of attaining possible happiness, or, at least, bearable existence. So those who are covered by a thick cloud of ignorance endeavour to amass more dream money, acquire more dream possessions, seek more dream pleasures in the many dream births and deaths. The Master directs us to work for the realisation of Truth, not through action but through knowledge, which is waking into our real Self, where alone true happiness can be found.

8. Like bubbles in water the universes rise from, dwell in, and dissolve into the supreme Self, their material cause and support.

9. The world of plurality is projected by the imagination upon the eternal, all-pervading Lord, whose nature is Existence-Intelligence, as are the varieties of ornaments upon gold.

10. Just as the all-pervading space appears many when it is associated with objects, so does the omnipresent Lord when in contact with the *upādhis* (adjuncts), and becomes whole (or alone, *kevala*) when these disappear.

11. Because of the contact of the Self with different *upādhis,* notions of caste, *āshrama,* colour, etc., are superimposed on it, as taste, colour, etc., on water.

Note: Bubbles, ornaments, divided space, etc., are familiar similes which Śaṅkara uses to illustrate more vividly the real nature of the world and its relation to its source and substratum, the Self. By introducing *upādhis* (adjuncts) he means that due to the numerous *upādhis* the one Self appears as the numerous *jīvas,* possessing numerous qualities and belonging to numerous castes, creeds, countries, etc. The Lord here is *Hṛṣīkeśa*, the Lord of the senses, which make us see *upādhis* (and world) in the imagination. His other name is Viṣṇu whose nature is Existence-Consciousness-Bliss. Let us not forget that all these superimpositions of worlds, senses, bodies, qualities, etc., take place only in the "imagination" of the Lord, as the *jīvas,* as they do in the dream state.

Space is infinite, but appears divided into bits because of the objects it contains, whose shapes it takes outwardly and inwardly. In a round pot, for example, it becomes round when it fills its inside, as its content, and limits its outside, as its container. In a square box it takes a square shape inside and a square shape outside. Thus, space, which is boundless, becomes limited to the shapes of the things that occupy it and that it pervades, but regains its limitlessness when the things are removed. Likewise, the infinite consciousness appears to be limited as the plurality of finite objects superimposed on it and recovers its infinitude when thoughts come to a stop, like the gold which returns to its original state when the ornaments made of it are melted.

To repeat: the common substance of all objects and the source of all qualities is the seeing mind, the omniscient and omnipresent Consciousness, Lord Viṣṇu, Brahman. This develops stanza 6, which makes the waking state a mere dream — a most perfect analogy, which equates the two states in all respects as objects, as actions, or as sensations.

12. Determined by past actions, and made up of the five great elements that had undergone mutual combinations and fivefold divisions is the (gross) body, the medium of experiencing pleasure and pain.

13. The five *prāṇās,* the ten organs, *manas* and *buddhi* formed from the original elements (before the

aforesaid combinations and divisions), constitute the subtle body, which is the instrument of experience.

14. The causal body is the beginningless inexplicable ignorance. Know the Self to be different from these three *upādhis*.

Note: These are the adjuncts which the Lord assumes, to which the previous stanzas refer. They are the three sets of bodies — the gross, subtle and causal — which veil the Self and which germinate from the seeds of past actions and thoughts, strictly according to the law of cause and effect or predestination — karma. (1) The *annamayakośa* — the sheath of food — is the physical body, evidently made of the five gross elements, namely, earth, water, fire, air and ether. (2) The *Sūkṣma śarīra* or subtle body is made of the five life-functions or *prāṇas*, which supervise the various activities of the gross body, the ten organs *(indriyas)* — five of perception, namely, eye, ear, nose, etc., and five of action, namely, hands, legs, etc. — *manas* (the thinking faculty) and *buddhi* (the reasoning faculty, or intellect). This subtle body includes the three sheaths known by the name of *prāṇamayakośa, manomayakośa,* and *vijñānamayakośa,* (the sheath of life, of thinking, and of reasoning respectively), and (3) the Causal or *ānanda-mayakośa,* which is made of the purest *sattva* and comes first in the manifestation of the qualities *(guṇas),* bearing within itself the seeds of all bodies as determined for each birth by the *jīva's* past actions. Hence it is identified with *avidyā,* the "indescribable ignorance," which prevents the *jīva* from cognising itself as the Supreme Self. Whilst all the other *kośas* (sheaths) subside or drop off at one time or other, say, in sleep, swoon, death, etc., this *kośa* alone persists throughout the long period of transmigration till *Videhamukti* (disembodied Liberation) destroys it altogether, as it does all future births.

The term "beginningless ignorance" needs some explanation. *Avidyā* is not beginningless for each particular *jīva*: it has a beginning as well as an end along with the causal body, or else there could be no Liberation. "Beginningless" refers to the *jīva*-formation in the Self, rather in the "imagination" of the Self (stanzas 9 to 11), which seems to be endless.

> 15. By associating with the five sheaths the pure Self appears to assume their nature, as a (colourless) crystal assumes the blue colour of the cloth that comes near it.

> 16. Intense reasoning separates the pure Self within from its sheaths, as rice is separated from its husk by pounding.

Note: Here we are shown how the Self falls into ignorance and how it extricates itself from it (stanza 4). Wrapping itself with the *upādhis* it has itself created, the Self begins to identify itself with them as the *jīva* or man. As it is devoid of qualities and pure by nature, it assumes the qualities of its *kośas,* like the crystal which assumes the colour of the object on which it is placed, or like the mirror which reflects the faces that stand before it. This causes it to fall into all sorts of delusions, most of which are contributed by the physical sheath on account of the sensory organs which are entrenched in it, and which perceive the physical qualities of the body and induce the thoughts "I am fair," "I am fat," "I am a woman," "I am Indian," etc., making it believe itself, the pure intelligence, to be the gross body, different from all other bodies, and liable to birth, disease, old age, and death, also to be cut, burnt, or buried. Wandering for a long time in the world of illusions and suffering the consequences of its ignorant actions, it finally wakes up to the realisation of its deplorable state and begins to reflect and discriminate, ending in the practice of *sādhanā* (spiritual discipline).

In his *Aparokṣānubhūti* Śri Śaṅkara says, "Knowledge cannot arise by any other means than by inquiry *(vichāra),* just as the sight of things is impossible without light" (verse 11). Constant inquiry into the nature of both, the body and the Self, ends by separating the one from the other, as pounding separates the grain from its husk, revealing the true nature of the Self transcending *avidyā.*

17. Although it pervades all things, the Self does not shine anywhere but in the pure intellect, like a reflection on a polished surface.

Note: To realise its true nature, not as bodies but as the life-intelligence which pervades them, the *jīva* polishes its intellect to such purity, through study and meditation, as to make it capable of reflecting the Self as in a mirror. For all the other functions of the mind are completely shut out from the direct contact with the Self: the senses, for example, perceive only physical qualities (shapes, colours, sounds, etc.), the aesthetic sense appreciates only sensible beauty, *manas* (lower intellect) deals only with the most superficial day-to-day business, memory brings back from the past events that had sunk below the threshold of consciousness, etc. All these have commerce only with the phenomena: the reasoning faculty alone, when highly cultivated is capable of turning towards the transcendental Self and eventually succeeds in reflecting it. The phenomena are the dust (the thoughts or imagination) that covers the spotless mirror of the Self. When the dust is wiped off by the strong brush of the inquiry, the experience will be the glorious Self and the state will be *samādhi*.

> 18. Know that the Self is ever like a king, distinct from the body, senses, *manas*, and intellect, which are matter *(prākṛti)* by nature. It is the witness of their action.

Note: The Self (as *jīva*) is supreme, the Lord of the *upādhis*, which He, as life, moves and works up and, as mind, cognises and directs. The *upādhis* — the bodies and all the processes of thought — are insentient "matter", and thus have neither will nor energy of their own to act and move on their own initiative. It is the

Self which moves them as it wills, like the mover of a puppet-show, himself remaining unmoved.

The distinction between the Lord and His superimpositions is obvious to everyone, for there is hardly a human being who has not seen a lifeless body to contrast it with his own and other living bodies. Life is the Lord. Its withdrawal leaves the body a corpse.

19. When the clouds move fast in the sky the moon appears to run. Likewise to the undiscriminating the Self appears to act when seen through the active sensory organs.

20. Depending upon the light of the Self — *Ātma Caitanya* — the body, senses, mind and intellect act in their respective fields, just as men work by the light of the sun.

21. Because they lack discrimination people superimpose on the immaculate Self, which is consciousness-existence, the qualities and actions of the body and the sense-organs, just as they superimpose blueness on the sky.

22. Through ignorance the actions of the mind *(manas),* which is an adjunct, are attributed to the Self, as is the movement of the water to the moon reflected in it.

Note: These four stanzas deal with action which is falsely ascribed to the Self. They insist that the Self does not act, being everywhere and alone existing, itself space and itself time, so that when we see hands, legs and tongues moving and think that their owner's self is acting, we are unwittingly superimposing action on the actionless Self, much as we superimpose blueness on the sky, which is colourless. The actions which are seen in the *upādhis* are dependent not on themselves but on the Self (or Life) which pervades them. Besides, as we have seen in the last Note, they are too insentient to be called the actors, much like the writing pen which cannot be called the writer, or the spectacles which cannot be called the seer. If neither the Self nor the body is the actor, who then is the actor? The following stanzas, especially 26, will give the answer.

23. Attachment, desire, pleasure and pain exist so long as thinking exists. When this ceases as in deep sleep, they too cease. Therefore they belong to the thinking faculty alone and not to the Self.

24. Just as radiance is the nature of the sun, coolness of the water, and heat of the fire, so is the nature of the Self reality, consciousness, bliss, eternity, purity.

25. By indiscriminately mixing up the Being-Consciousness of the Self with the modification of the intellect, the notion "I know" arises.

26. The Self does not act, nor is the intellect intelligent, but the deluded *jīva* imagines himself the knower and seer.

27. As the man who mistakes a rope for a snake is overcome by fear, so is he who mistakes himself as (the limited) *jīva*. He regains fearlessness who realises himself not as *jīva* but as the supreme Self.

Note: These stanzas summarise what has gone before. The nature of the Self is bliss, eternity, purity, etc. It can have no desire, attachment, pain, jealousy, hatred, or fear to act. These arise not in the pure Self but in the self which has turned into a deluded *jīva* as the result of its thinking in the waking state. I said waking state, for thinking ceases in deep sleep and with it cease desire, attachment, etc., i.e. the *jīvahood*, only to restart on the return to the waking state. "Therefore they (attachment, desire) belong to the thinking faculty alone."

To repeat, the *jīva* is the Self which, in the waking, got mixed up with thinking on one hand and with the inherent sense of 'I' on the other and has acquired the impressions 'I am this body,' 'I am born,' 'I am afraid,' 'I am ill,' 'I am different from all other men' etc. It is evident that the changes in these impressions do not cause corresponding changes, nor an increase or decrease, in the *jīva's* real nature, which remains always the supreme Self itself, but in its thoughts, notions, ideas.

Stanza 26 reiterates the statement that the Self does not act (stanza 21), but, when it comes under the influence of the *upādhis* and gets deluded, it believes itself to be an actor, desirer, knower, etc: it assumes a fictitious aspect which is neither purely sentient as the Self, nor purely insentient as the intellect, but an anomalous combination of both and bears the name of "ego" or "*jīva*", which imagines itself to be the body, i.e. mortal and exposed to all sorts of danger. Like the person who develops fear at the sight of a snake which is nothing but a rope, the *jīva* develops evil propensities due to this notional error till it wakes up to the realisation of itself as the limitless, fearless, indestructible Self.

This stanza clearly determines the identity of the actor and declares him to be the imaginary entity who vanishes the moment a serious investigation is carried out in his real nature. His actions are likewise imaginary. Thus the Self is inactive in its real nature, but imaginarily active when it falls a prey to the *upādhis*.

28. Just as a lamp illuminates a pot, so does the Self illuminate the intellect, the sense-organs, etc. These, being insentient, cannot illuminate themselves.

29. A light needs no other light to reveal it; so the Self, being knowledge itself needs no other knowledge to be cognised.

Note: The insentience of the *upādhis* continues to be the subject of discussion. 'Illuminate a pot' means rendering it visible. In darkness no object can make itself be seen without a lamp. But a lamp wherever it may happen to be can be seen by its own light. The senses (and the body), like the objects, have no light of their own by which they can be known. A knower, who is the light as well as the seer must be present to reveal them. The eye through which the seer sees, for example, is insentient and does not see anything in his absence, as in sleep or in a swoon. Similarly for thinking a thinker is necessary, the intellect, being a mere function of the mind, is as insentient as the eye. But to know the knower no other knower is needed, himself being knowledge, and this is evident to all men, for there is no one who is not sure of his own existence, as 'I', without the necessity of being told of it by others.

> 30. By rejecting the *upādhis* with the help of the scriptural dictum 'Not this, not this' the identity of the *jīva* with Brahman, as denoted by the *Mahāvākya* (the Great Text 'I am Brahman') is realised.

Note: This stanza begins the teaching of *sādhanā,* the practice by which Brahman can be realised. Brahman is the knower, or Self, mentioned in the last stanza. The practice is rejection of anything that is not Brahman through investigation. It stands to reason that since the Self is pure sentience, pure knowledge, all insentience must be considered as superimpositions on it and, thus, eliminated. The bodies (or *upādhis*) are well known to be insentient, so that by rejecting them the investigator will find himself left as the only logical residue. This is the realisation of the *Mahāvākya* 'I am Brahman' in one's actual experience. The *kaivalya* (aloneness) of *suṣupti* (dreamless sleep), which is devoid of *upādhis*, is the support and proof of this *Mahāvākya* (see stanza

57 and Note) for all men and *Turīya* or *samādhi* for the Self-realised yogi.

31. Being born of ignorance, all the perceived objects, like the body, etc., are as perishable as water bubbles. Realise yourself to be the immaculate Brahman, entirely different from all of them (saying).

32. I am different from the body and, thus, free from the changes of birth, old age, decay and death. I have no relation with the senses, like sound, etc., for I am devoid of sensory organs.

33. I am different from the mind and, hence, free from sorrow, attachment, aversion and fear, for the scriptures describe the Self as devoid of breath and mind, pure, etc.

34. I am attributeless, actionless, eternal, free from thoughts and dirt, changeless, formless, ever liberated, ever pure.

35. Like space I pervade all things outside and inside. Immutable, ever the same in all, pure, unattached, stainless and motionless am I.

36. I am verily that supreme Brahman, which is eternal, pure, free, one, unbroken bliss, non-dual, true knowledge and infinite.

Note: It is evident that these *ślokas* expound the *Mahāvākya* 'I am Brahman,' of which stanza 30 speaks both negatively and positively, so that by constantly dwelling on its nature, the meditator may grow to intuit the consciousness or intelligence that is himself shorn of the *upādhis*. The true 'I' — the Self — is *guṇa-less, upādhi-less* and thus boundless, infinite. But when it assumes the *upādhi,* it limits itself to their qualities *(guṇas).* All attributes are conditioning: when we say, for example, that Venkatesan is dark or thin, we limit Venkatesan to the colour, breadth and height of his body, and also to the limited average period of the human life, and no more. Whereas the real Venkatesan is the "stainless, motionless, changeless, infinite and eternal intelligence."

The first three of these stanzas not only distinguish between the seer and his *upādhis,* as stanzas 18 and 30 do, but deny even the existence of any relation between them (32). For what relation can there be between the spotless spirit and the totally inert matter. The apparent relation they imply, is entirely illusory, like the relation of a dreamer to his dream body, which is completely nonexistent. It can now be easily seen that the 'Neti, Neti' method given in the previous stanzas forms the negative part of the *sādhanā,* which discards the insentient superimpositions, whereas the one given here forms its positive part, which affirms the reality of the subject himself as "the one, unbroken, non-dual bliss and knowledge." The next stanza develops the point:

37. The impressions caused by constant meditation on 'I am Brahman' eventually annihilate ignorance and

all its offshoots, like the medicine that radically annihilates the disease.

Note: Whether waking or dreaming, whether we perceive external objects or internal sensations, we are in contact with nothing but impressions or ideas, that is, with the contents of our minds alone. Sri Ramana Maharshi calls them in one word, "thoughts." All our actions, possessions, human relationships, conceptions, all the objects we perceive through the senses and all emotions consist of nothing but thoughts, emanating from our own consciousness.

This stanza enjoins us to substitute these thoughts, which are as empty and fugitive as the moving air, and which perpetuate ignorance, by those of 'I am Brahman.' By constantly asserting oneself to be the absolute Consciousness lasting intuition of the nature of the Consciousness is created in the mind which will end in direct experience of it, destroying *avidyā* root and branch, like the medicine that cures the disease and all the suffering it causes.

It will be noticed that this stanza does not speak of "transforming" the mind into Brahman, for the mind (not *manas* but *Cit)* is Brahman itself, which has no need to be transformed into itself once again. What some yoga literature means by transforming it is that when the *upādhis,* which are perceived through ignorance, cover it, the mind appears as if it is the *upādhis* themselves and thus needs to be transformed into Brahman. Actually it is at no time other than Brahman, whether in the beginning, in the end, or in the middle, like the sun which ever shines whether it is hidden from our vision by clouds or not.

38. Retiring to a solitary place, abandoning all desire, and controlling the senses, meditate with an unswerving attention on the one infinite Self.

39. The wise man should mentally sink the entire objective world into the Self, which he should visualise as spotless as the sky.

40. Having abandoned everything — form, caste, etc. — he who has realised the supreme Self abides in the very fullness of consciousness and bliss.

41. The distinctions of knower, knowledge and known do not exist in the supreme Self, which being of the nature of knowledge and bliss, shines by itself alone.

Note: The topic is still the method of Realisation. Meditating on 'I am Brahman' alone will not produce significant results if it is not accompanied by renunciation of the non-Brahman — all objects of sense and all mental habits — to impart to the mind the requisite polish, tranquillity and fervour to pursue the practice relentlessly, or else not only the meditation will soon become an intolerable burden, but the latent instincts will assert themselves and will drag the practitioner back again to his old way of life.

It stands to reason that to produce the *kaivalya* of *suṣupti* in *jāgrat* all superimpositions have to be held back. Only then the clear sun of the being will shine in all its splendour. As for solitude, it is absolutely necessary for clear reflection, though it is discouraged in the case of the aspirant who is not yet ready for it. The solitary place which the Master recommends must be entirely free from human and non-human disturbance. Generally speaking, human association has again and again proved to be detrimental to clear meditation, if not in the beginning, at all events after some time, more so if it includes the opposite sex. Too long familiarity with people of different emotional, intellectual and spiritual make-ups tends to stimulate criticism, disagreement, and disharmony, if not also active hostility. In cases where human company is very *sāttvic* (pure, harmonious), like that of the Guru and of most congenial *sādhakas*, it is very desirable, for it supports the practitioner at the time of spiritual crises and physical ailments and needs.

Stanza 41 speaks of the negation of the distinction between knower, knowledge and known. We have partly dealt with this point in the Note to stanza 5 (q.v.). It is axiomatic that when everything turns into its real nature, namely, consciousness, all divisions and, therefore, all objectivity ceases and the state is called *samādhi*, wherein the pure being-consciousness-bliss that is oneself "shines by itself alone."

42. When contemplation is constantly churned in the *araṇi* of the Self, the flame of knowledge which is spared by it will burn all the fuel of ignorance.

43. When knowledge scatters the darkness (of ignorance), the Self spontaneously reveals itself, as does the sun when the light of the dawn scatters the darkness (of the night).

Note: In olden days to light a fire an *araṇi* was used. This consists of two pieces of wood joined together and hollowed in the middle, into which a wooden rod (or pestle) was inserted and turned round and round to produce sparks by friction. Constant churning of the *vichāra* (inquiry) burns away the thinking processes, leaving the mind, the substratum of thought, pure by itself — self revealed — which is *Jñāna,* the supreme Knowledge. *Jñāna* rising, *avidyā* vanishes, like the night's darkness at the approach of the dawn, bringing the *sādhanā* to a close and heralding the final Liberation, nay, it is Liberation itself.

44. Although the Self is ever present, it is not realised because of ignorance. On the destruction of ignorance it appears as if (newly) realised, like the ornament on one's neck.

45. Individuality *(jīvahood)* appears in Brahman through delusion, like the appearance of a man in a post (in the dark). It vanishes the moment its real nature is realised.

Note: The topic of the methods of attaining *mukti* (salvation) which started in stanza 30, having finished, the *Ācārya* reverts to the subject of *avidyā* (ignorance), which causes the Self to forget itself but from a new angle. We have to conclude from these stanzas that the terms, Liberation, Self-quest, Self-realisation, etc., used here and in other *Vedāntic* works are a misnomer: they are made for the convenience of the seeker who sees things from the sensuous level; for in reality the Self is at no time bound to be liberated, or absent to be searched for, like the proverbial necklace which is thought to be missing, but has actually at no time left the Princess's neck. The *avidyā* in which the common man is sunk arises from his confusion about his own identity, of which he is sure in general but exhibits a lamentable ignorance when he attempts to work it out in detail. In a sensible world where he sees himself only as a body, among an infinite number of bodies, he hardly notices the distinctive phenomenon of thought, which he takes to be natural in a human being. It is only after contacting superior intellects through study and *satsaṅga* (good, wise company), and after reflecting over the whys and wherefores of things, that is, when he begins to think for himself that he bumps against the mind as an element in his constitution to be accounted for. Then he awakes to the probability of his 'I' being more mind than body. The realisation that they are only mind, or consciousness, and naught else comes to the very few as an immediate, indubitable experience at the end of a *sādhanā* that has gone on for years, if not lives, when the delusion will break along with their *jīvahood* for ever, like the thief that has been discovered by the light of a lamp to be a mere wooden post. Even the body (and the world) will then prove to be mindstuff.

> 46. The knowledge that results from the realisation of the nature of the Reality instantly destroys the ignorance evidenced by the notions of 'I' and 'mine', like the removal of the confusion about one's direction.

Note: The individuality or *jīva* is non-existent. With the rise of knowledge ignorance and the 'I'-sense which results from the 'I-am-the-body' notion and causes the sense of separateness from other bodies, are 'instantly destroyed'. Although the senses are primarily at fault in creating the impression of differences, the imagination perpetuates it in the memory, and nothing can destroy it but the enlightened Guru, who acts like a signpost that guides the traveller in a foreign land.

> 47. In his supreme vision *(Jñāna Cakṣu,* or eye of wisdom) the perfected yogi sees the whole universe in, and as, his own self.

> 48. The whole universe is verily the Self: nothing exists other than the Self. As pots are nothing but clay so all things appear (to the yogi) to be made of the Self.

Note: This is the experience of the Reality by the one who has lost his 'I' — and 'mine' — sense, i.e., his sense of separateness. He sees not only himself but also the whole universe as the pure mind, so that nothing exists but mind. The *Māṇḍūkya Upaniṣad* identifies Aum with "all this," i.e. the phenomena with their seer, like identifying the various ornaments with the metal gold out of which they are made or the pots with the clay out of which they are baked.

49. Endowed with Self knowledge, the liberated soul discards the characteristics of the *upādhis* mentioned before, and, as he is by nature *sat-cit-ānanda,* he remains only that, like (the maggot that has grown into) a wasp.

Note: The identification with the *upādhis* ceases at the dawn of Self-realisation. Although the yogi may continue to be in the same body, saddled with the same *upādhis*, either to teach the truth to those who are prepared to follow in his footsteps or just to live till the end of the *prārabdha* of the body, he remains in the enjoyment of the bliss of his own divine nature, resembling the wasp that has released itself from the characteristics of its old maggot state.

50. Having crossed the sea of delusion and killed the monster 'likes and dislikes', the yogi, now one with peace, delights in the glory of his own self.

51. Having given up attachments to transitory external pleasures, and, being satisfied with the joy within, he shines inwardly like a light inside a jar.

Note: The monster 'likes and dislikes' represents the pairs of opposites in creation. The perception of a kaleidoscopic variety not only obstructs the oneness of life from our vision, but also creates attraction for some objects and repulsion for some others, both of which enhance delusion and bondage, and, therefore, mental disquiet. The yogī who has realised the one Self in all things has automatically rid himself of this disquiet and retains, in the waking state, the peace of the being within, the peace which everyone enjoys in dreamless sleep.

Like "light inside a jar" is very expressive. No one can see the lamp which is hidden inside a pot, yet the pot remains inwardly lighted. The man who is permeated with the glow of the supreme Experience alone perceives and enjoys this blissful light within himself. Outsiders remain blind to it and may not even guess its presence, though it shines like the sun in the yogi's heart, the yogi's own consciousness.

52. Though associated with the *upādhis,* the all-knowing sage *(Muni)* remains like the ether, uncontaminated by them. He moves about like a madman unattached as the air.

53. When his *upādhis* are destroyed, the *Muni* merges completely in the all-pervading Lord, like water into water, space into space, and light into light.

Note: Stanza 52 clarifies stanza 49. The *Muni* is the *Jīvanmukta* who has attained Liberation, but continues to be in a body till it drops off at ''death", when he is said to have attained *Videhamutkti* — disembodied Liberation — and has completely merged into Lord Viṣṇu, the pure *Satcidānanda* Brahman, like light into light, etc. Yet, although with a body, the *Jīvanmukta* experiences the state of *Videhamukti* in his daily life at will. Vidyāraṇya writes that "in him arises the condition which is like the Liberation after dissolution of the body," and that the difference between *Jīvanmukti* and *Videhamukti* consists that in the former senses and mind are present, but in the latter they are not. Thus the *Muni*, while still in a body, knows the exact state in which he will be after "death" and enjoys its bliss even now.

By "he moves about like a madman" is not meant that all the *Jīvanmuktas* behave like madmen, unattached to home, caste, community, etc. That some *Muktas* (liberated men) did actually wander about like madmen, at least in olden days, does not make it a rule for all *Muktas* to do so, for we know many of them to have been outstanding teachers of this supreme science, who lived in fixed establishments surrounded by thousands of disciples. Some others lived in palaces, unknown to ordinary men, for not every *Mukta* is destined to be a teacher or wanderer. The majority, whose "light is hidden inside a jar," lead a normal life, unrecognised by even their most intimate relatives and friends. In fact *Bhāgavata Purāṇa* recommends the last form of life for them to shelter them from the amorphous, spiritually vacuous crowd, who visit saints in hopes of material benefits, or from the materialists who are apt to rail at them as frauds, leaving the *adhikāri* (mature seeker) to find his way to them by a subtle intuitive attraction.

As for the *Muni* remaining uncontaminated by the *upādhis*, Vidyāraṇya quotes the *Śrutis* to describe the *Sthitaprajña* (he who is steady in the supreme Knowledge) as "Though with eyes, he is, as it were, without eyes; though with ears, he is, as it were, without ears; though with mind, he is, as it were, without mind; and though with life, he is, as it were, without life." *(Jīvanmukti Viveka)*

54. Know that to be Brahman, the gaining of which leaves nothing more to gain, the enjoyment of which leaves no other enjoyment desirable, and the knowing of which leaves nothing more to know.

55. Know that to be Brahman the perception of which leaves nothing more to perceive, the cognition of which leaves naught else to cognise, and which, having become, one returns no more to birth.

56. Know it to be Brahman that which fills all quarters — above and below — which is Existence-Consciousness-Bliss, non-dual, infinite, eternal and one.

Note: This description of Brahman negatively depicts the complete freedom, self-sufficiency and blessedness of the perfect state, which, once attained, no further dependence on, and enjoyment of, the unreal world will be desired. Even the taste for scientific knowledge, which is so highly valued in this sputnik-age, will be lost. So will also be lost the love for all earthly achievements, though the *Muni* may even appear to be interested in them. All worldly pleasure is counteracted by displeasure being founded on blind infatuation, lust, greed, false values and false expectations; there is no enjoyment which remains an unmixed blessing to the end. Love of enjoyment is an infectious state of the lower mind which grows with indulgence undermining the peace and welfare of the enjoyer. A well-known Socratic dictum runs that "Pleasure is a nail which nails and rivets the soul to the body, until it becomes like the body," that is, insentient, dead to the life of the Spirit, in which alone undiluted happiness can be realised.

That Brahman "fills all the quarters," we have already seen that the state of being has no need for space, nor for time, nor for number, for it is "one" only, does not act, and it alone exists.

> 57. Know it to be Brahman that which is indicated by the *Vedānta* (as the residue) after that which is not or which has been negated *(neti),* and which is the one immutable, indivisible bliss.

Note: The *Neti, Neti sādhanā* mentioned in stanza 30 by which every percept and concept, every sensible object and thought is rejected as unreal, leaves Brahman as denoted by the *Mahāvākya* as the residue, namely, as the pure mind into which all of them rise and by which they are perceived. To a question by Parīkṣit as to how the *Śrutis* describe the limitless and indescribable Brahman, Śuka reports the deities in charge of the *Śrutis* to answer, "By simply negating the limited world as not Brahman" *(Bhāgavata,* XI), implying that the residue of the negation will be the negator himself, the Brahman which is massive bliss. This is corollary to stanza 30, which establishes the identity of the *jīva* with Brahman after the *upādhis* have been eliminated (by *sādhanā).*

58. Depending on only a particle of that which is of the very nature of unbroken bliss (Brahman), Brahma and the others enjoy it proportionately.

Note: Every sentient being is Brahman, whose nature is sentience and infinite bliss. Therefore, all beings bear in themselves the potential bliss of the Infinite, which is fully realised in *samādhi,* but which the gods, humans and sub-humans, even ants and worms, partially enjoy as sensuous experiences, proportionately to their degrees of manifestation of sentience. Thus all worldly happiness and pleasures are fleeting reflections of that inherent bliss of the Self, like the happiness experienced in dreams, which appears to come from external objects, but actually emanates from the dreamer's own being.

59. All things are united with That; all actions are made possible by That: Brahman, therefore, permeates everything, like butter in milk.

Note: In "All things" are included thoughts, actions, emotions, etc., which, although are countless and differ in qualities from one another, they are united in the subject (Brahman or "That"), their container and from whom they emanate. Because he is one and indivisible, the integral unity of the multiplicity is made possible in him, their Source. Hence the subject pervades all things — objects, actions, events, sensations, time, space, etc., "like butter in milk."

60. Know that to be Brahman which is neither subtle nor gross, neither short nor long, birthless, changeless, formless, casteless, nameless, and free from qualities.

Note: Śaṅkara has already amply dealt with the nature of Brahman — what it is and what it is not — especially in stanzas 31/36. Here he wants to stress the fact that Brahman is devoid of every vestige of attributes, albeit it is the source and ground of all attributes *(guṇas).* The attributes or qualities are finite and changing whereas Brahman is infinite, changeless and eternal. We saw how the phenomenal Venkatesan (Note on 31/36) is limited in every way because of his consisting of nothing but qualities, whereas the intelligence who uses that name and qualities is the pure Brahman, birthless and deathless.

61. Know that to be Brahman by whose light the sun and the others (stars) are illuminated, but which is not illuminated by them, and due to which all things shine.

62. Brahman pervades the entire universe outwardly and inwardly and shines by itself, like the fire which permeates the red-hot iron ball.

Note: The description of the indescribable Brahman continues. "All things shine" means "appear to a knower." Nothing can be said to exist without an intelligence to be aware of it. That intelligence is Brahman. None of the billions of stars with all their glory and millions of universes know the mind, but the mind knows them all. No part of the body — heart, liver, lungs, head — knows the mind, which works through and permeates them, but the mind knows each and every one of them.

Stanza 62 appears to be in part a repetition of stanza 59, but actually it has a high significance to the yogi whose attention is fixed on the pure Consciousness, which he sees, like space, permeating the inner and outer parts of all things without losing its radiance or identity. Therefore even the suns and universes are Brahman in substance, like the red-hot iron which has no heat other than that of the fire which pervades it.

> 63. Brahman is other than the universe. Apart from Brahman nothing exists. Should anything appear so to exist, it is as unreal as a mirage.

> 64. All that is seen or heard is not other than Brahman. Through knowledge of the Reality, the universe appears to be the non-dual Brahman, which is Existence-Consciousness-Bliss.

Note: "Brahman is other than the universe," seems to contradict the previous as well as the following stanzas, but the author is still thinking of the "outwardly" and "inwardly" of the previous stanza which he wants to develop further. He means that if we take the universe to be actually as it appears to us (externally), as the millions of qualities we perceive through our senses in it, it is not Brahman at all, for Brahman, as we have again and again studied, has no qualities whatsoever. And stanza 64 stresses this idea, namely, that nothing that comes through the sensory organs — eyes, ears, etc. — is real.

But if we take the universe as phenomena, as impressions or appearance in the consciousness and originating from it (internally), then it is the consciousness itself, and, thus nothing exists but consciousness — Brahman.

Evidently this non-dual vision, the oneness of both the internal and the external, will not be had except through the immediate apprehension of Brahman.

> 65. Although the Self is Being-Consciousness and omnipresent, it is perceived only by the eye of knowledge *(Jñāna Cakṣu),* and not by that of ignorance, which is like the blind eye that cannot see the ever-radiant sun.

> 66. Heated in the fire of knowledge, which is kindled by hearing (the scriptures), etc., the *jīva* cleansed of its impurities, shines by itself like gold.

Śaṅkara is now leading us to the climax, namely, Self-realisation, which is the sole aim of this treatise. To recapitulate he reverts to the original idea that ignorance can be killed only by knowledge, which begins with devotional practices, *satsaṅga* (company of the wise), study of the Scriptures, etc., when the cleansing process commences, like the fire which begins with a mere spark and ends in a great flame, the flame of knowledge, which is the direct perception *(Jñāna Cakṣu)* of the self-revealing Reality.

> 67. The Self which is the sun of knowledge, rising in the ether of the heart, verily dispels the darkness (ignorance), pervades and sustains all things, shines by itself and makes everything shine.

Note: This is Self-realisation proper. The *jīva* which has been purified by penance and practice now perceives itself as the absolute, immaculate consciousness, shining like the sun in the ether of the heart, wherein all universes are created and supported. In writing this Śaṅkara must have had in mind the two beautiful *ślokas* of the *Cāndogya Upaniṣad* which read:

"Within this habitation of Brahman (the body) there is a lotus-like chamber, and within it a minute vacuity. What is within this is worthy of search."

"Verily as space is boundless, so is the ether within the heart. Both heaven and earth, fire and air, the sun and the moon, also lightning and the stars, and whatever is, as well as whatever is not in the universe — all are within this vacuity." (I, iii, 2-3)

This amounts to saying that the boundless space which we see outside us is nought but the "ether" of our own hearts in which all the perceived and unperceived objects and universes are accommodated and that therefore there exist no such things as external. When the illusion of externality breaks in Self-realisation, all forms, solidity, plurality, and all the products of the *guṇas* (qualities) at once dissolve leaving a single, homogeneous substance, namely, "the sun of knowledge which shines by itself and makes everything shine."

> 68. He who renounces all action and worships in the holy shrine (lit. *tīrtham* or sacred water) of his own Self, which transcends directions, time and space, is omnipresent destroyer of the pairs of opposites, eternal bliss and stainless. He becomes all-knowing and attains immortality.

Note: Renunciation of action and self-dedication to the *sādhanā* and quest after this knowledge of the Self are, again, the heart's cry and farewell message of the Master to the fervent disciple. They are the twin lights which guide the latter in this uncharted land of the Spirit to the triumphal crescendo which rises from the first steps of the *sādhanā* to the glorious consummation of *Mukti*, which is the Supreme Liberation and, therefore, the Supreme Bliss.

INDEX

A

A—Vaiśvānara, first state of wake-fulness 50, 51
— *Vaiśvānara* or *Viśva* 39
Absolute, approach to 18
Ācārya 55
action (karma) 58
— as the promoter of ignorance 59
— desireless; 59
— renunciation of 59
— ascribed to Self 69
activities, belong to *jīva,* not to Supreme Self 70
adhikāra (full maturity) 39
advaita 60
affliction of ignorance 9
ajapa 8
ākāśa (heart) 15
annamaya kośa — sheath of food 65
aparokṣānubhūti 67
araṇi, metaphor of 79
āshram 2, 12
association, — with the opposite sex to be avoided 78
Ātmabodha 55 ad infinitum.
ātma-caitanya (light of the Self) 69
Ātman (= Self); 49, 52
— as single as Aum 15, 35, 38
Aum 37, 38
— three pādās of 48
— as Viśva, Taijasa, Prājña 48
— as consciousness 49
— identity of 49
— different sounds of 49
avidyā (primeval ignorance) 2, 55, 60, 66

B

Being, aloneness of 5
Bhagavad Gītā 5, 12, 26, 58
Bhakti (devotion) 52
bliss,
— of absolute knowledge 55
— of absolute truth 55
— Supreme 92
body,
— gross divisions of 65
— subtle, constitution of 64, 65
— causal 65
— three sets of 65
— causal constituents of 65
— physical, made of five gross elements 65
— a corpse 69
Brahman, infinite consciousness, absolute knowledge 40
— sat, cit, ananda 82
— description of 84
— sentient being as 87
— nature of 87-90
— attainment of 91
— concept of 75
Brāhmana 3
Brahmarṣi 28
Brahmavidyā 31
breath-control (prāṇāyāma),
— as the means of stabilising the mind 18
— use of 18

C

Caitanya (pure consciousness) 15
cerebral cells 8
Chāndogya Upaniṣad 91
Christian extremists 12

Cit (pure mind) 15
commentaries 56
concentration 15
consciousness,
— simple 48
— superimposed upon consciousness 62
— supreme 61
— constant churning of 79
culture, extroverted 1
— intellectual 1

D

devotee, destiny of 13
devotion 32
dhyāna (meditation) 3, 7, 18, 59
— method of 9
— causes of failure 9
dhyānic current 7
dhyāna-yoga 18, 21
disciple, qualified 1
distinction,
— absence of 51
— between knower, knowledge and known 78
divine grace 20
dreams, empty of substance 43
dreamless sleep 6, 44, 73, 83
drink, pure 25
duality, of subject and object denied 61

E

Electicism 13
emancipation 35, 58
Enlightened Ones 32
environment, proper 11, 21
ether, of heart 15, 91

Existence, single 30
experience, sensory 20
— triple 52

F

faith 3, 32
family life, not hindrance to Sādhanā 28
— complexities of as hindrance to Sādhanā 29
feeding, indiscriminate 24
food, availability of 25
— animal 25
— climatic and constitutional conditions in 25
— sāttvic 24
— effects of sāttvic 24
— served in Āśramas, temples and Brahmin houses 25
Fourth, the state of realization 35, 39, 47, 49
frenum lingui 8

G

Gauḍapāda 35, 36
Gauḍapāda Kārikās 35
Gauḍapāda and Śaṅkara 36
Guru 2, 9, 11, 13, 14, 17, 19, 27, 29, 31, 78, 81

H

Hari, Supreme Brahman equated with Aum 40
harmony, ways of achieving 26
health, sound — necessary for sādhanā 24, 25
heart 8, 14, 15, 22, 23, 28, 32, 83, 91
Hindu extremists 12
Hṛṣikeśa, lord of senses 63

I

I, identification of with the body erroneous 17
— search for the root of the I sense 17
— infinite and intelligent 18

ignorance 55
— removal of 56, 58
immortality 56, 92
impressions 55
India, a land of miracles 21
— Vedāntic 21
individuality (jīvahood) a delusion 79
infinitude, how to recover 64
inquiry (vichāra) 17, 67, 68, 79
intellect, as mirror 67
— turning to transcendental Self 68
intoxicants, prohibited 25

J

Jāgrat, waking state 7, 39-42, 44-46, 51, 78
Japa, repetition of a mantra 7, 8
Jīva, individual self 39, 60, 61, 66-68, 70-73, 81, 90, 91
Jīvanmukta 13, 23, 44, 83
— a state of experiencing vague, shapeless dreams 44
Jīvanmukti, Self-realization 23, 84
Jīvanmukti-viveka 85
Jñāna, supreme knowledge 2
— knowledge of Reality 21, 58, 79
Jñāna-Cakṣu, direct perception 81, 90, 91
Jñānendriyas, instruments of knowledge 43
Jñāni-siddhas 21

K

Kaivalya, aloneness of the pure Being 6, 16, 39, 45, 50, 73
Kaivalya of Suṣupti in Jāgrat state 78
Kaivalya Upaniṣad 31
Karma 58, 59
karmendriyas, instruments of action 43
kataka 60, 61

knowledge
— of the Absolute Supreme 56
— path of knowledge 5
— inadequate, as the cause of failure 9
— knowledge 55-60, 62
— as destroyer of action 58
— as purifier of jīva from ignorance 60
— as path of Self realization 17

L

law, immutable, natural 19
— of cause and effect 65
laya 8
Liberation 3, 6, 32, 43, 55, 57, 58, 79, 83, 84, 92
light, within the heart 83
liquor, injuries of 24
lord, Blessed 31, 32
— with adjuncts *(upādhis)* 63, 65
— and his superimpositions 69
— as life 69

M

M-Prājña 39
— a state of deep sleep (suṣupti) 51
Mahāvākya 52, 73, 74, 86
Mahāyānists 22
Man, distinguished from body 45
— lord of all 46
Manas, thinking faculty 16
— as lower intellect 68
Māṇḍūkyopaniṣad 35, 36
Māyā 20
meditation 9-19, 32, 77
ad infinitum.
memory, harmful to Sādhanā 14

mind, nature of 13
— how to control 15
— distinguished from *manas* 22
— as self 60
— as waves 60
— concept of 61
mind control 7
mind transformation 10
miracle 21
miracles and visions 21
mukti, liberation 13, 29
— method of attaining 77, 92
Muktikopaniṣad 35
multiplicity, merge of — into unity 45

N

Neti, Neti sādhanā 86
— negative formula to explain Self 75
nirvāṇa 22
nivṛtti 11

O

Objects, gross 58
occultism 2
Organs of perception 65
Organs of action 65

P

pādās, feet, quarters 40
Purīkṣit 87
Paramātman, Supreme Self 15
Patañjali 8
penance, tapas 12
pitfalls 20
prānāyama, breath control 18

prājña 42
— a state of deep sleep 44
— a mass of consciousness and bliss 45
— gateway to knowledge, a merger of waking and dream states 45
predestination — karma 65
Practice pre-*samādhi* 22
Puruṣa, the Most High 32

Q

qualities (guṇas) products of 65, 92

R

Ramana, Maharshi 17
ratiocination 60
realization, through knowledge 62
— final 67
— method of 77
Reality 16
redemption 9
regularity 26
renunciation of action 92
Ṛṣis, Self-realized sages 1

S

sādhakā, a practising yogi 8
— life of a 11, 12, 20, -s
— disciples 27, 28, 31
sādhanā, spiritual discipline 2
— necessity of 5
— non-dualistic discipline 6
— discipline of the mind 6, 9, 13, 14
— complexities of family life as hindrance to 28, 60, 67
— as the means of Self-realization 73
— positive part of 75, 92
samādhi 7, 22, 23, 61, 68, 87

Sāṇḍilya Upaniṣad 15
Śaṅkara 3, 40, 55, 57, 62, 67, 88
sannyāsa, renunciation and asceticism 4
sannyāsi, world renouncer 1
sat-cit-ānanda, existence, consciousness and bliss 16
sthitaprajña, steady in the supreme knowledge 85
scriptural dictum: "not this, not this" 73
Self
— presence of 41
— nature of 77
— finite, infinite 59
— as sun 61
— contact of — with upādhis 63
— how to separate — from five sheaths 66
— assumes the qualities of kośas 66
— in association with five sheaths 66
— as transparent in intellect 67
— superimposition upon 69
— vis a vis upādhis 68
— as jīva, lord of upādhis 68
— as, distinct from matter 68
— as witness 68
— as actionless 70
— as jīva 71
— as reality-consciousness, bliss, eternity, purity 71
— inactive in real nature but imaginarily active when associated with upādhis 71
— as light 72
— as illuminator 72
— as pure sentience, pure knowledge 73
— identification of — with jīva 66
Self-knowledge 55
self-purification 13
sheaths (kośas) 66

siddhis, psychic powers, display of
— harmful 21
— distinguished from occultists 21
skulls 20
sky, superimposition of blueness on 70
sleep 45
society, avoidance of 78
spirit, land of 15
spiritual life 11
spiritual urge 17
Śruti 15, 55, 85
stage of apprenticeship 11
states, three 7
— symbolised by Aum 40
substance, single 30
Śuka 87
sun of knowledge 92
supersensuous, hearing and seeing 21
supreme knowledge 57, 58
Supreme Self, apprehension of 47
suṣupti, dreamless sleep 7, 39, 45, 50, 73
svapna 39
— a state of perceiving internal objects 43
Śvetāśvatāra Upaniṣad 6

T

Taijasa, as second pāda 43
tapas, austerities 43
tapasvin 12
teacher 3
theology 2
truth 2
turīya, fourth state 7, 35, 39, 40, 42, 46, 47, 48, 51, 52, 74

U

U — Taijasa 39, 49
Universe, as Self 81
— as bubbles in water 62
Upadeśasahasrī 4
upādhis 68, 72
— insentience of 72
— nature and place of 75
— absence of relation between — and Self 75
upāsanā, external worship 19
— becomes Self-worship = para bhakti 19
uvule 8

V

vairāgya, detachment 14
Vaiśvānara 39, 41
vāsanās, age-long propensities 57
Vedānta 2, 55
Vedāntic tradition 24
Vedic Invocation 37
vegetarianism, in Brahmin and non-Brahmin communities 25
vichāra 8, 59
vichāra and dhyāna 18
videhamukti 66, 84
Vidyāraṇya 84, 85
vision of Reality 8
Viṣṇu — Existence, Consciousness, Bliss 63
Viśva 39, 42, 46

W

Waking state, state of thinking 6
— compared to dream state 62
— a mere dream 64
water-sponge metaphor 18

wheel, of birth and death 55
— of pleasure and pain 55
world
— as a shadow play 20
— a dream 62
— of plurality 63
— of illusions 67

Y

yoga 15, 32
— dangers of 21
— of renunciation (= sannyāsa yoga) 32
Yoga Vāṣiṣṭha 59
yogi 13, 35, 56, 82
— as ether 83
yogic practice 2, 20
— fantastic notions of 20

Z

Zen 60
Zen Buddhists 22